BLOW
WIND

ALSO BY DANIEL MACDONALD

A History of Breathing
MacGregor's Hard Ice Cream and Gas
Pageant
Velocity
Bang

Plays for young adults
(written or co-written by Daniel Macdonald)

Flock Formations
Tragedie
Waking
Blind Love
These Things I Know
The Romeo Project
HERE
Radiant Boy

DANIEL MACDONALD

WITH MUSIC BY EILEEN LAVERTY

PLAYWRIGHTS CANADA PRESS

TORONTO

First edition: September 2022
Printed and bound in Canada by Imprimerie Gauvin, Gatineau

Jacket design by Kisscut Design

Playwrights Canada Press
202-269 Richmond St. W. Toronto, ON M5V 1X1
416.703.0013 | info@playwrightscanada.com | www.playwrightscanada.com

LIBRARY AND ARCHIVES CANADA CATALOGUING IN PUBLICATION
Title: Blow wind / Daniel Macdonald ; with music by Eileen Laverty.
Names: Macdonald, Daniel, 1962- author. | Laverty, Eileen, 1966- composer.
Description: A play.
Identifiers: Canadiana (print) 20220251509 | Canadiana (ebook) 20220251541
  | ISBN 9780369103635 (softcover) | ISBN 9780369103659 (PDF)
  | ISBN 9780369103642 (HTML)
Classification: LCC PS8575.D6296 B56 2022 | DDC C812/.6—dc23

Playwrights Canada Press operates on land which is the ancestral home of the Anishinaabe Nations (Ojibwe / Chippewa, Odawa, Potawatomi, Algonquin, Saulteaux, Nipissing, and Mississauga), the Wendat, and the members of the Haudenosaunee Confederacy (Mohawk, Oneida, Onondaga, Cayuga, Seneca, and Tuscarora), as well as Metis and Inuit peoples. It always was and always will be Indigenous land.

We acknowledge the support of the Canada Council for the Arts, the Ontario Arts Council (OAC), Ontario Creates, and the Government of Canada for our publishing activities.

Canada Council Conseil des arts
for the Arts du Canada

ONTARIO ARTS COUNCIL
CONSEIL DES ARTS DE L'ONTARIO
an Ontario government agency
un organisme du gouvernement de l'Ontario

Canada

ONTARIO | ONTARIO
CREATES | CRÉATIF

To Melanie

LEAR: Doth any here know me? This is not Lear.
Doth Lear walk thus, speak thus? Where are his eyes?
Either his notion weakens, his discernings
Are lethargied— Ha! Waking? 'Tis not so.
Who is it that can tell me who I am?
FOOL: Lear's shadow.

—William Shakespeare,
King Lear Act I, Scene 4

CORDELIA: Sir, do you know me?
LEAR: You are a spirit, I know. Where did you die?
CORDELIA: Still, still, far wide.

—William Shakespeare,
King Lear Act IV, Scene 7

FOREWORD

BY ANGUS FERGUSON

It's always an adventure developing a new play with Daniel Macdonald. A wonderful journey toward discovering nuggets of truth and then building a solid structure that can hold them. Learning how to adjust the perceptive lens until the characters come into sharp focus. Talking for a long time. As a dramaturge and director, knowing when to ask questions and when to shut up. Sensing when it is time to bring in other elements such as music, design, other collaborators, and actors who can make the written words vibrate in the air. *Blow Wind* was a challenging and rewarding example of this; a fulfilling pilgrimage from the first step until a destination was reached. Thank God theatre has deadlines, because once you are inside the journey it would be easy to keep going forever.

The initial starting point came from a conversation between Dan, Skye Brandon, and myself. "What about a modern version of *King Lear*, but set on a prairie farm?" If you are going to draw from a source, then it seemed like a good idea to draw from the best. Shakespeare's ideas are still a fertile pasture to graze in. This initial idea was a simple first step. Then the real journey began.

Buried in that initial idea was one of the most important elements of this play, which was that it was born directly out of a geographical place. On one level *King Lear* is about land. Dancing Sky is a small theatre in the village of Meacham, Saskatchewan—population eighty-seven souls nestled in the vast expanse of the Canadian prairie. We are surrounded by an endless sea of farmland. Dan had sat in our audience many times and had built a clear sense of this community. He was intent on talking directly to us, telling a story that we would connect with in a very personal way, and telling it in a language we would understand.

In *King Lear*, the aged monarch is handing over his kingdom to his three daughters, who each want a bigger piece of the pie, but the realities of the contemporary family farm are very different. The truth is that even though most people in rural Saskatchewan have a deep connection to a family farm, a farmhouse, or the old homestead, and that many have had this connection for three of four generations, these connections and memories are emotional and romanticized. Everyone wants to go home to the family farm and have a fall feast or Thanksgiving supper, but fewer and fewer young people want to take on the tasks, risks, responsibilities, and sheer hard work of running a family farm. More and more of them are moving to the city. Small family farms are becoming rarer, with large corporate farms becoming much more common. The story of *Blow Wind* holds this truth. We want to feel the connection to the land, but the modern world is calling us to live somewhere else. So, the idea of passing the land on to the next generation but remaining connected is a conundrum.

The other thread suggested by *Lear* was that of the deterioration of memory and mental faculties as we age. Dan and I both had experiences of family members struggling with the onset of dementia, and it seemed like a very powerful, relevant, and fertile field to explore. Theatre seemed the perfect medium to investigate the fluid vagaries of dementia and the grey borders that grow between what is "real" and what is not. Dan is a writer who knows how to wield the power of theatre to explore the fluidities of time and place. I love working with writers who recognize and utilize the unique powers of live theatre.

As the story and characters grew, it also became clear that this was a very contemporary story about a family that has travelled in different directions to follow their own personal narratives. The modern world often demands that we travel and move great distances to follow our dreams and goals, often away from "home" and family. The play asks us to consider our connections and responsibilities to place, memories, and each other.

As I said, *Blow Wind* grew out of a very specific place and from a particular group of people. Due to that, it feels very honest. Over the years I have learned that plays and stories that are very specific tend to also be the most universal because of the honesty they contain. We had a wonderful time growing and cultivating this play in the heart of rural Saskatchewan. I hope that it resonates and finds new places to grow and ripen all around the world.

Thanks for the journey, Dan.

Angus Ferguson is a theatre director, designer, dramaturge, and teacher who is dedicated to creating art and developing artists in Saskatchewan. He is the founding artistic director of Dancing Sky Theatre in Meacham, where he develops and produces new plays. He teaches at the University of Saskatchewan Drama Department and at St. Peter's College in Humboldt, just to see if he can preach what he tries to practise. He lives in the small village of Meacham, Saskatchewan, with his wife, dog, cat, and a garden that is far too big.

COMPOSER'S NOTES

When director Angus Ferguson asked if I'd be interested in working on a project with Dancing Sky Theatre, of course I said yes! I have long been a fan of the work Angus produces in his theatre in Meacham, Saskatchewan. He wanted me to meet Daniel Macdonald and discuss the possibility of writing music for a play. Now, I should mention I had no previous experience in theatre, so I wasn't quite sure how all the parts would fit together, but from the very first meeting with Angus and Dan, I was certain I was beginning a new creative process with two of the very best.

I suppose I'd expected to receive the finished play and begin work on the music. It was far better than that. From that first meeting, through many discussions and drafts, I watched Dan's characters and story evolve. To have an ongoing artistic conversation as a creative partner is a rare gift; it is both exciting and daunting. But there was so much inspiration from which to draw upon for the songs. The actors generously and warmly invited me into their space and provided further inspiration. What impressed me most was Angus and Dan's trust in the process, and in me, and their unwavering faith that the muses would deliver.

From the table readings, rehearsals, director's notes, to opening night and the final bow, I enjoyed every moment! I am most grateful to have had this opportunity to learn, collaborate, and work with such talented and lovely people.

Thank you to the original cast: Cheryl Jack, Mark Claxton, Kate Herriot, Darla Biccum, and Marcel Petit. Thanks also to Jensine Emeline Trondson; Louisa Ferguson and the staff at Dancing Sky Theatre; Cheryl Thorson, Greater Saskatoon Catholic Schools, Jesse Brown, and Greg Hargarten. Special thanks to Angus for the invitation and for your guidance throughout. And to Dan for welcoming me into your creative process and sharing this journey with me.

Blow Wind was originally commissioned by Dancing Sky Theatre in Meacham, Saskatchewan, and was first produced by Dancing Sky Theatre in April 2018 with the following cast and creative team:

Kathleen: Cheryl Jack
Steven: Mark Claxton
Jolene: Darla Biccum
Tom: Marcel Petit
Sarah: Kate Herriot

Music and songs composed and performed by Eileen Laverty

Director: Angus Ferguson
Stage Manager: Jensine Emeline Trondson
Set Design: Angus Ferguson
Lighting: Angus Ferguson, Jensine Emeline Trondson
Costumes: Louisa Ferguson and the company

A second production of *Blow Wind* was produced at the Station Arts Centre in Rosthern, Saskatchewan, in June 2019 with the following cast and crew:

Kathleen: Cheryl Jack
Steven: Cam White
Jolene: Michelle Piller
Tom: Daniel Knight
Sarah: Lauren Marshall

Director: Daniel Macdonald
Musical Director: Alison Jenkins
Composer: Eileen Laverty
Technical Director: Craig Langlois
Set and Lighting Design: Derek Butt
Costume Design: Nicole Zalesak
Stage Manager: Jensine Emeline Trondson
Station Arts Director of Operations: Josie LaChance
Station Arts Director of Programming: Nicole Thiessen

Blow Wind received workshop development through the Saskatchewan Playwrights Centre.

WRITING DENOTATIONS

An ellipsis (. . .) denotes the character's speech trails off.

A word or punctuation in parentheses ( ) denotes that this is probably what the character intends but does not speak what is in the parentheses out loud.

A forward slash (/) within a character's line of dialogue indicates where the next line of dialogue should begin.

An em dash (—) denotes that a character's speech is cut off.

The original production was set in the round with all actors always slightly visible with the exception of the actor playing Kathleen, who entered and exited to the wings.

The original production at Dancing Sky Theatre in Meacham, Saskatchewan, had one singer/guitar player who performed all of the songs solo. The second production at the Station Arts Centre in Rosthern, Saskatchewan, featured all of the actors singing and playing musical instruments (except the actor playing Kathleen). This published version of the play features the actors singing and playing instruments like in the second production.

Theatres wishing to feature one singer/guitar player only must request permission and obtain an alternate draft of the play directly from the playwright.

The play has one intermission. Each act runs approximately fifty minutes.

CHARACTERS

Kathleen: mater (sixty-eightish)
Steven: eldest sibling
Jolene: a year and a bit younger
Tom: adopted son, a few years younger than Jolene
Sarah: youngest sibling, a few years younger than Tom

The four siblings are also known as "The Ensemble."

ACT I

In a small light, SARAH *steps to the piano and begins to play.*

KATHLEEN *enters. She sees* SARAH *and they smile at each other.*
KATHLEEN *sits with* SARAH *at the piano. She plays a few simple
chords with* SARAH. *As she does, the others enter one by one and
either watch or play along.*

Partway through, KATHLEEN *abruptly stops. Everyone stops.*
KATHLEEN *picks it up again and the others join. But she stops
again, holding the moment. Everyone holds their breath and waits.*

*She starts again then stops. She can't remember. She tries one
more time but stops mid-phrase, frozen. Finally, she gets up and
exits, slightly puzzled but not upset. The siblings watch her go.
They glance at each other.*

The lights fade as KATHLEEN *exits. A slightly different instru-
mentation kicks in.* SARAH *moves from piano to guitar. The
piano is pushed up stage by* TOM. STEVEN *plays his guitar.
Perhaps* TOM *joins.*

JOLENE
*We met in the springtime, we danced through the summer
The memories I fondly recall
The music and laughter
And dreams ever after
And I loved you best of all.*

The singing stops but the playing continues as SARAH steps forward.

SARAH
Just over there is the tire swing that we climbed and fell off of when we were little. It's still clinging to the biggest elm on the farm, but the rope has stretched and the tire kind of just drags in the dirt. Even the grand-kids are too old for it. It kind of just sits there, waiting.

JOLENE
And over there's a little broken-down house from the old farmstead. The first in this whole place. It stands like a memory. Came before we did and got grey and bent just like the farmers who owned it. They sold the land to my dad and moved to town.

SARAH
This is my sister, Jolene.

JOLENE waves or something.

JOLENE
This is my sister, Sarah.

STEVEN
I remember we'd play there and laugh and pretend it was haunted. But we never went there past sundown.

SARAH/JOLENE
This is my bro—

SARAH
This is my brother Steven.

STEVEN
And over there is a copse of trees where we'd play until mom would ding the dinner bell and yell for us, and over there is the Quonset, and

right over there is our lane that takes us to the road that takes us to the highway that takes us to town that takes us to a bigger highway that takes us to the city or further if we have the need.

TOM
I wandered the hills, to the banks of the river
I searched o'er the valley, the wind had taken me there
Take me to the music, let me hear the laughter
Of my love so rare.

SARAH
And this is Tom.

JOLENE
Our adopted brother.

SARAH
Sure, but we never call him our—

JOLENE
Tom runs the farm.

TOM
Well, the farming part.

SARAH/STEVEN
Slowly fading colours led to the lonely white of winter
Why we parted I cannot recall
But the music's still playing
And the dreams are far from fading
And I still love you best of all.
And I still love you best of all . . .

> *The song doesn't come to an end. Instead, as tough they are*
> *caught off guard,* KATHLEEN *steps to downstage centre and looks*
> *out. The song trails off or stops and they look at her for a moment.*

JOLENE
And over there—

But SARAH interrupts her.

SARAH
Over there is my mom, Kathleen.

> *JOLENE looks at SARAH for a moment. There is a pause, a moment, as KATHLEEN stands there and they all look at her in anticipation, and then a shift. All but SARAH find their spots and SARAH steps into the scene as it begins.*

> *KATHLEEN starts yelling and flailing her arms.*

KATHLEEN
Blow winds! Blow! Rant! Rage!

> *SARAH shouts over KATHLEEN's rants. The storm begins.*

SARAH
And on the day I come back, I find her standing in a field on the back quarter of our farm yelling with all her might into a ferocious, thundering storm.

> *The ensemble create a ferocious thundering storm. They make as much noise as they can—mouths, instruments, anything.*

KATHLEEN
What'd you say, storm? I can't hear you? Shout! Louder! Thunder, is that all you got? You think you can beat me!?

> *SARAH shouts over the storm:*

SARAH
This is the storm that my mom is screaming at as I stand not ten yards away trying to get her attention. Thunderous noise, lightning, buckets of rain.

The storm goes on without KATHLEEN *shouting, then . . .*

But this was what's really there.

The storm immediately stops. Instead, the ensemble creates
the most peaceful tone possible. Delicate picking, birds singing,
maybe a frog or cricket, wind whistling through branches.

A beautiful sunny day in October. Quiet. Barely a breeze. A field in
the middle of the day on our family farm. Both standing in thick, grey
clumps of hardened soil. And my mom. Yelling to the heavens.

KATHLEEN
You can throw anything at me and I won't go down! Come on then!
Try! Come and wash me down the back quarter, off the farm, and onto
the road! Go ahead!

The ensemble stays. They maintain the "nice day" sounds.
SARAH *steps into the scene with* KATHLEEN.

SARAH
Mom?

KATHLEEN
Is that what you want? Here I am! You think I can't handle this?

SARAH
Mom! Are you okay?

KATHLEEN *turns to look at* SARAH.

KATHLEEN
I don't want to see you right now! You've got some nerve! I don't want
to see you; I don't want to talk to you!

SARAH
What? Why?

KATHLEEN *(to the storm)*
What. You gonna take the farm from me too?

SARAH
Mom? Kathleen? It's—

KATHLEEN ˙
Go back to the house, Robert. Just go back to the house!

SARAH *(to us)*
Doesn't see me at all. She's seeing Robert, her dead husband. My dad.
She's in the middle of a raging storm, a perilous night of her own
creation. And I'm Robert. She sees Robert. To her it looks something
like this:

> *Suddenly we are seeing things from* KATHLEEN's *perspective
> again. The storm rages again.* SARAH *becomes Robert.*

(as Robert) Kathleen. Kat. Are you okay?

KATHLEEN
Leave me alone.

SARAH *(as Robert)*
Come on back to the house.

KATHLEEN
You're worse than the wind! You're going to destroy this too!

SARAH *(as Robert)*
Kathleen.

KATHLEEN
How could you do this, Robert? How could you?!

SARAH is closer now but still Robert, comforting her.

SARAH *(as Robert)*
Shhhh. Kathleen.

KATHLEEN
It's all washing away. All our work. All our—

SARAH *(a bit of Robert, a bit of SARAH)*
Kathleen. It's me.

KATHLEEN quiets and is breathing now as though she is somewhere between that world and this. She begins to listen. The sounds quiet. SARAH stays.

Mom?

KATHLEEN breathes heavily and looks at SARAH.

KATHLEEN
What.

SARAH
You okay?

KATHLEEN
I'm . . .

KATHLEEN takes a long look at SARAH.

You're not . . . you're not . . . Sarah

SARAH
No, Mom.

KATHLEEN
You're . . .

SARAH
Sarah, Mom. I'm Sarah.

KATHLEEN
I know / who you are.

SARAH
Your daughter, / Mom.

KATHLEEN
I know. Sarah.

> *A moment as* KATHLEEN *composes herself. She starts to realize she's not where/when she thought she was. She looks around.* KATHLEEN *looks at the sky, the land, trying to make sense of this . . .*

SARAH
Mom?

KATHLEEN *(snapping a bit)*
What.

> SARAH *doesn't respond.*

What? . . . What? I said what.

SARAH
You okay?

KATHLEEN *(defensive)*
Are *you* okay?

SARAH
What?

KATHLEEN
Nothing.
I'm fine. Just. I'm just looking at my fields.

SARAH
We were on a field in the back quarter. It'd been fallow for a couple of years.

KATHLEEN
Three.

SARAH
What?

KATHLEEN
Three years. Fallow.
I was watching the fox. She's back.
Started seeing her a few months ago.

SARAH
Her?

KATHLEEN
I was following her, but I lost her. I think she went to the hill.

SARAH
Hill? What hill?

Now KATHLEEN's not sure what hill.

KATHLEEN
I mean to the edge. Of the field. The aspens along the road. So I stopped here. Remembering.

Pause.

I'm going across the field to the road.

SARAH looks out.

SARAH
Okay. I'll come with you.

They don't move.

KATHLEEN
When did you get back?

SARAH
Just . . . just now. You weren't at the house so—

KATHLEEN
I was remembering that storm.

SARAH
That why you were shouting?

KATHLEEN
What?

SARAH
Nothing. What storm?

Another pause. Maybe KATHLEEN looks around again.

KATHLEEN *(slightly amused)*
Not sure if I was in my right mind just now.

SARAH
Ha. When's anyone ever in their right mind?

KATHLEEN looks at her daughter. She smiles, warms.

KATHLEEN
You came back.

SARAH
Yep.

KATHLEEN thinks, looks around again.

KATHLEEN
How are things?

SARAH *(not okay)*
Okay.

SARAH looks out to the fields, the house.

You're sure you don't want to come back to the house? Maybe we can walk to the aspens tomorrow. Jolene's worried about you.

KATHLEEN
Jolene's always worried about me.

SARAH
Well she wants to / make sure you're—

KATHLEEN
There's one that's always in her right mind.

SARAH
Yeah, well—

KATHLEEN
She's planning a supper. She tell you?

SARAH
I know. That's why / we have to—

KATHLEEN
No. Not for tonight. A supper. Like a feast supper. A dinner supper.
This weekend. Steven's even coming.

SARAH
Oh wow. Like a dinner? Why's Steven coming? Why's she /
planning a—

KATHLEEN (*thinking about something else now*)
Your father never planted enough aspens.

SARAH
(???)

KATHLEEN
Look. Back toward the house. Gaps. Along the lane. They're not spaced
right. Not even, or something.

Pause.

SARAH
You sure you're okay? Maybe we could walk back to the house together
/ and have some supper . . .

KATHLEEN (*somewhere else again*)
God, look at that sky. You know, there aren't a lot of places in the world
where people just stand around and look at the sky.

They look some more.

Sky's always bluest in the fall.

SARAH
You used to say that when I was a kid.

KATHLEEN
Robert would say it. He loved this field for the sun.

SARAH
Isn't the sun / pretty much the same any—

KATHLEEN
When I couldn't find him, I'd come out here. He'd be standing in the field, crop or no, just looking around. He even danced with me a couple of times out here. Maybe right here . . .

In the darkness STEVEN *begins to pick something on the guitar.*

. . . He'd sing, I don't know, Engelbert Humperdinck, or . . . the Carpenters.

*Someone sings a bit of "Close to You" by the Carpenters
. . .* KATHLEEN *dances quietly to herself.*

SARAH
Then why don't you plant anything in it?

. . .

Mom?

The memory fades. KATHLEEN *gives her daughter a brief look.*

KATHLEEN
We should go back and eat. I know Jolene's got to go.

SARAH
Oh. Okay.

KATHLEEN
The supper's for me.

SARAH
You? Why?

KATHLEEN
Well it's for me, but it's not really for me.

SARAH
Who's it for then?

> *Scene shift. The music ends abruptly.* JOLENE *enters. They all walk into the kitchen mid-scene as though in mid-conversation.* JOLENE *is moving around the kitchen cleaning up or setting the table.*

JOLENE
Barley. He planted mostly barley there.
That where you found her?

KATHLEEN
She didn't "find" me. That's where I was.

> *There's a flurry of activity as* JOLENE, *keeping busy, goes about getting supper ready for* KATHLEEN.

JOLENE
Mom doesn't let Tom plant that field. Do you, Mom?
(to SARAH) You staying for supper?

KATHLEEN
I have my reasons.

SARAH
Where else would I eat?

JOLENE
You never know.
Was she hard to find?

KATHLEEN
I'm right here, you know.

JOLENE
You are now. That's 'cause I sent Sarah to go find you.

KATHLEEN
I'd have come back. I know my own farm.

JOLENE
I'm not going to eat with you tonight, Mom. Sarah's here so she can
stay and eat supper with you.
(to SARAH) Haven't eaten with my own family all week.

SARAH
How are they?

JOLENE
Good. Good. Kaitlyn and Brandon are good. They're both busy with
school and everything.

KATHLEEN
Kaitlyn's a very good hockey player.

SARAH
And how's Brandon?

KATHLEEN
Brandon's a very good video-game player.

JOLENE
Good. Good. He's—everything's good.

SARAH
How's Roy?

JOLENE *(giving up nothing)*
Good.

SARAH *(to audience)*
Roy's Jolene's husband.

JOLENE *(to audience)*
He sure is.

> *JOLENE puts something down or hands something to SARAH as if to go.*

Good luck.

KATHLEEN
I'm right here.

JOLENE *(to SARAH)*
It's getting difficult to—
(now to KATHLEEN) It's getting difficult to leave you alone for long stretches of time, Mom.

KATHLEEN
It is not.

JOLENE
Yesterday you were halfway down the road and Tom found you and brought you back in his truck. Do you remember that?

KATHLEEN
I like getting rides in his truck.

JOLENE
He told me you said you were going to the rink.

KATHLEEN
What if I was?

JOLENE
But you weren't going to the rink, mom. We both know that.

KATHLEEN
I *was* going to the rink.

JOLENE
But you had no reason / to go to—

KATHLEEN
I was still going to the rink.

JOLENE *(sighs)*
Anyway. Mom, why don't you go wash up? I need to talk to Sarah.

KATHLEEN *(walking away)*
About me.

A pause as JOLENE *stops and waits till* KATHLEEN's *gone.*

JOLENE
You got my email?

SARAH
Your text? The length of three emails? Yes.

JOLENE
Yeah. She's . . . there's no way of knowing one hour to the next where she's at.

SARAH
I'm here now. I can keep an eye on her.

JOLENE
I don't mean out there, I mean in here *(indicates her head).*

How long you here for?

SARAH doesn't really know.

Chris stayed in Ontario?

SARAH nods.

SARAH
I found her yelling at a storm just now.

JOLENE
Uh-huh.

SARAH
Uh-huh?

JOLENE
As in, she does that.

SARAH
Why?

JOLENE *(shrugs)*
It's new. She's been doing it a few months.

SARAH
Months? What's it about?

JOLENE
(No idea.)

SARAH
She's yelling at dad. She kept calling out "Robert."

JOLENE
Well if you'd been married to someone for forty-five years, you'd probably yell at them too.

SARAH
She was . . . she was pretty angry.

JOLENE
Yeah. Well. He wasn't always a picnic.

Another moment.

It's getting worse.

SARAH
That's what you said / in your email.

JOLENE
She's young.

SARAH
I know.

JOLENE
It could go on for years.

SARAH
I'm not going anywhere.

JOLENE eyes SARAH.

JOLENE
What do you mean?

SARAH
I'm here.

JOLENE
To stay?

Pause.

SARAH
I left Chris.

JOLENE
Left? Like, left left?

SARAH shrugs.

Like divorce left?

SARAH *(shrugs)*
Well I couldn't stay in Brantford.

JOLENE
Isn't that where you live? Don't you have a job in Brantford?

SARAH
Sort of. Sometimes. Part-time.

JOLENE
So what'd he do?

SARAH
What?

JOLENE
He cheat on you?

SARAH
No.

JOLENE
Hit you? He didn't seem like the / kind of guy—

SARAH
No, he didn't hit me.

> Pause. JOLENE *is waiting for* SARAH *to elaborate.*

JOLENE
(????)

SARAH
I don't . . . I'm not—

JOLENE
Welfare? Homeless? Gambling? Heroin? Mafia?

SARAH
No! Okay? It's nothing like that.

JOLENE
Then tell me what the—

SARAH
I don't know, okay? It's hard to explain. Things just felt
. . . shaky? Okay?

JOLENE
Shaky?

SARAH
Like, not firm. Not solid. I didn't know what we were doing. Like I was
always guessing what was happening, what was like, next. Or something. Then we had this big fight and . . . and I left.

JOLENE looks at her.

JOLENE
A fight.

SARAH
Yes.

JOLENE
You had a fight.

SARAH
Yes. A big fight.

JOLENE
A big fight.

SARAH
And I sent you that email and then you texted me and I thought I
should—

JOLENE
I didn't text you to leave your husband 'cause you had a fight!

SARAH
I'm here, okay? I'm here! Never mind why or what's going to happen.
I'm here and I want to help and I want to stay here, okay?

JOLENE
For the record, I never asked you to come. Right? You messaged me
and I told you how things were . . . how things were.

SARAH
I know.

JOLENE
So now you're going to plunk right down here and—and do what?

SARAH
Help.

JOLENE
I've been managing.

SARAH
Yeah, by skipping supper with your family.

JOLENE
Yeah, well, they skip supper with me all the time.

SARAH
What about Steven?

JOLENE
What about him?

SARAH
Does he ever come to help?

JOLENE
He lives in Calgary.

SARAH
So? I live in Ontario.

JOLENE
I don't think he has any immediate plans to leave his wife and come hang out. And you know what he's like.

SARAH
I do?

JOLENE
It's hard to get him to, you know . . . he doesn't visit often.

SARAH
What's up with this supper thing?

JOLENE
Who told you about the supper?

SARAH
Mom.

    Pause.

What. Is it a secret?

JOLENE
No. Course not. We're having this supper. Like a retirement supper. For, like, to honour Mom. Steven's coming.

SARAH *(tentative)*
Okay.

JOLENE
And Steven and I have been talking and, like, now that you're here, there's . . . um . . . things that need to get sorted out before . . . before . . .

SARAH
Before what?

JOLENE
Just before. Mom. You know.

SARAH
Like what?

JOLENE
I don't know! Just, like, everything, okay?

> SARAH *looks to the audience while* JOLENE *goes about doing kitchen stuff.*

SARAH
This is the way Jolene talks all the time. "We need to." "You need to." She looks at the world in absolutes. In imperatives.

JOLENE
You need to go check on Mom.

SARAH
Okay.

> JOLENE *watches her go as she stays busy. A pause. She looks to the audience. Her turn.*

JOLENE
That's not fair. I wouldn't say "you need to" or "we need to" if people didn't need to do things. Sarah just needs to—

She pauses, catching herself.

Sarah has never felt that she "needed" to do anything. Life just unfolds for Sarah. When she was little, Mom would make me take her to the rink to skate? I'd put her skates on, tie 'em up nice and tight, and put her on the ice. She'd skate to the middle and sit down and just watch the people go round. For like twenty minutes. It's cute when you're four. When you're eight or nine it's just . . . weird.

    SARAH *is back.*

SARAH *(knowing)*
Who you talking to?

JOLENE
Mom coming down? Food's getting cold.

SARAH
In a minute.

JOLENE
What was she doing?

SARAH
Laughing at the mirror.

JOLENE
(See?)

SARAH
I washed her hands.

    JOLENE *sighs and leaves.* TOM *begins to play, dreamlike.*

    We are now with KATHLEEN *at the mirror. The mirror is a window to the yard as* KATHLEEN *stands over the kitchen sink washing dishes.*

KATHLEEN *(laughing)*
That was a good try, sweetie! Maybe don't try to swing as hard and you won't fall. Maybe Steven won't hit it so hard. Steven, that's not what a badminton racket is for . . . Well, it makes you look like you've got little squares all over your face . . . I know, it's a bit windy for badminton today . . . Well, you have to kind of predict where it's going to come down . . . Yes, Steven, just like seeing into the future.

> SARAH *appears in the light as a five-year-old. She's doing twirls with a baton, badly.*

SARAH
Look, Mom!

KATHLEEN
That's really good, sweetie. Look, you guys, Sarah's twirling the baton.

> JOLENE *appears with a badminton racket.*

JOLENE
She doesn't even know how.

KATHLEEN
Jolene.

JOLENE
That's really good, Sarah. Want me to show you some things?

SARAH
'K.

KATHLEEN
Anyone seen Tom anywhere?

> STEVEN *is there with a badminton racket.*

STEVEN
He's with Dad.

KATHLEEN
Where'd they get to?

JOLENE
No he's not. He went out to the trees.

KATHLEEN
What trees? By the road?

STEVEN
The trees trees.

KATHLEEN
Way out there? By himself?

JOLENE shrugs as she hits an imaginary birdie.

STEVEN
Dad gave him a hammer and some nails.

JOLENE
He's been dragging wood he took from the woodpile.

KATHLEEN
How's he getting the wood out there?

JOLENE
Carries it.

STEVEN
No he doesn't. He takes his bike and his wagon.

KATHLEEN
Across the fields?

STEVEN
Wagon tips over a lot.

SARAH
Looka me, Mom!

KATHLEEN
Sarah, stop hitting yourself with the baton.

JOLENE
Mom, she's gonna break it!

KATHLEEN
Someone should go find Tom. Jolene, where are you going?

JOLENE
To find Tom.

KATHLEEN
Well you need to go get your father.

JOLENE
Steven can get Dad.

STEVEN
No, you. I'll find Tom. I know where he goes.

JOLENE
I wanna find Tom.

KATHLEEN
Jolene, you go find your father.
(watches) Jolene, come back. You don't need to both go. Sarah, you stay here.

SARAH
I wanna go too.

KATHLEEN
Well you don't all need to go. Sarah? Sarah, come back. Jolene, you tell—

Pause.

You don't all have to go.

Pause.

Robert! Robert, tell the kids to come back to the house. It's supper.
Robert?
Jolene?
Tom? Tommy? Where'd you?
Sarah? Sarah?
Where—

A pause. A slight fear comes into her voice as if she can't quite see as clearly. The music fades. The others fade.

Robert?
Sarah?

SARAH is now there in the present.

SARAH
Yeah, Mom?

KATHLEEN turns, startled.

Everything okay?

KATHLEEN
Robert.

SARAH
Sarah, Mom.

KATHLEEN stares at her, trying to gain her wits.

You were calling me. Is everything okay?

KATHLEEN
Supper's ready.

SARAH
That's right. How did you know? Jolene made some scalloped potatoes with ham and carrots, I think. We kept it warm. Come on downstairs.

KATHLEEN
I don't understand.

SARAH
What, Mom?

KATHLEEN
Why she keeps making me scalloped potatoes.

They move to the kitchen. STEVEN is there. He catches SARAH by surprise.

STEVEN
It's true. She does.

SARAH
Holy shit! Steven. You scared the shit out of me. You don't yell? Or knock?

STEVEN
Nope. Wanted to surprise you.

They hug the obligatory family hug while they talk.

KATHLEEN
Hi, Steven.

STEVEN
Hi, Mom. It's Steven.

He gives her a hug.

KATHLEEN
I just said, "Hi, Steven."

STEVEN
She's gotten a little more confused of late.

KATHLEEN
I'm right here.

STEVEN *(ignores his mom)*
I heard you were back.

SARAH
Wow. Word travels. I got back three hours ago.

STEVEN
Jolene.

They smile knowingly. He looks toward KATHLEEN.

She okay?

SARAH
She's fine. She was . . . she was calling for me.

STEVEN
And Dad. Dad's not here, Mom. Dad's not here.

KATHLEEN
I know he's not here. Why would I think—

> STEVEN *tries to brighten the mood. During the conversation* KATHLEEN *stands there, bored. Every so often she attempts to do something to alleviate the boredom. Could be anything.*

STEVEN
But Sarah's here! Sarah's back.

KATHLEEN
Uh-huh. She's right there.

STEVEN *(to* SARAH*)*
How's things?

SARAH
Okay. Good. Fine.

STEVEN
Good.

> *A slight awkwardness.*

How long are you here for?

SARAH
Um . . . for like, / a while.

> *Beat.*

STEVEN
What's it been? Five years?

SARAH
Well 'cept for Christmas that time.

STEVEN
Is uh / . . .

SARAH
Chris?

STEVEN
Yeah. Chris. / Is he . . .

SARAH
He's still in Ontario. He's . . . uh . . . he's still / in Ontario.

STEVEN
Oh. Okay. Mom? What are you doing?

KATHLEEN
There's something in my slipper

Beat. STEVEN *turns back to* SARAH.

STEVEN
Are you guys, like, / what are you . . .

SARAH
We're separated. Sort of. / Well I—sort of separated from him for a while.

STEVEN
Oh.

Pause.

Oh. Okay. Gotcha.

Beat.

So, like, you've been married for / like, what, a . . .

SARAH
Two years. We—we've been married for two years.

STEVEN
Two years.

SARAH
Yep.

A moment.

STEVEN
You didn't see it comin'?

SARAH
What / do you mean?

STEVEN
'Cause we all, / like, knew—

SARAH
How's the boys?

STEVEN
Good! Awesome. Lucas is fourteen.

SARAH
Oh my God, fourteen?

STEVEN
Yeah. Good hockey player. Some scouts are lookin' at him.

SARAH
Scouts? Really? The Boy Scouts of Canada are looking—

STEVEN
Ha ha. Very funny. Hockey scouts.

SARAH
At fourteen?

STEVEN *(showing a pic from his phone)*
Yep. Goin' on twenty. Ha ha.

SARAH
And Bobby?

STEVEN
Good. Good.

　　Bored, KATHLEEN *starts to walk away.*

SARAH
You didn't bring the family?

STEVEN
Nah. Too busy. Mom. Where you going?

　　KATHLEEN *stops.*

KATHLEEN
I want to move the piano.

STEVEN
You need special movers to move / a piano, Mom.

KATHLEEN
I want to move it across the room, stupid.

STEVEN
Mom. We moved it last time I was here. Me and Lucas moved it to the sitting room. Remember?

A silence as KATHLEEN *contemplates this.* SARAH *breaks it.*

SARAH
You staying for supper?

KATHLEEN *(scoffing to herself)*
Do I remember.

STEVEN
Hmm? Tonight? No, I'm meeting some friends at the bar. Like Greg and Alex and those guys.

KATHLEEN *(half to herself)*
You need to stop asking me that.

SARAH
You staying here?

STEVEN
Here?

SARAH
The house? Our house? Our family's house?

STEVEN
Mom. Maybe put that down. No, I'm staying at Greg's.

SARAH
Oh. So, you're not / gonna stay at the house?

STEVEN

Greg invited me / and he's got this awesome home theatre system, like surround sound and all that . . . so . . .

SARAH

Oh yeah, for sure. No, yeah, I totally / get it.

KATHLEEN

Yeah, sure. Totally get it.

STEVEN

We were going to watch / the game and you know . . .

  Pause.

SARAH

Oh yeah. Totally. Totally.

KATHLEEN

Yeah, totally.

SARAH

See you tomorrow?

STEVEN

Yep. I'm gonna take Mom around and do some errands for the supper and stuff. Mom, I'm going to take you around tomorrow and / we'll like do errands and stuff.

KATHLEEN

Yes. I heard you when you told Sarah.

STEVEN

Cool. Okay, see you guys tomorrow.

KATHLEEN
Literally five seconds ago.

SARAH
Okay. Later.

STEVEN
Bye, Mom.

KATHLEEN
Okay, bye, Steven.

He leaves. SARAH *and* KATHLEEN *stand there for a moment.*
KATHLEEN *looks at* SARAH.

He's not here for the supper.

SARAH
What do you mean?

KATHLEEN
Jolene asked him to come. For the land assessment.

KATHLEEN *sits down to eat. She looks at her food.*

Scalloped potatoes.

STEVEN *and* TOM *have picked up guitars and start to play in
semi-darkness.*

SARAH
I'm seeing it.

JOLENE *begins to sing from a spot in the shadows even as* SARAH
steps into the light with her mom.

JUST OVER THERE

JOLENE
I should walk away, don't know why I stay
I have left so many times in my mind.
Just a stroll down the lane that leads to the highway
And leave this tired place behind.

KATHLEEN
What was the name of our first dog? That shepherd–collie cross? He was so sweet.

SARAH
At first I didn't notice anything different—

KATHLEEN
I can't find my . . . my . . . the thing I carry things in. You know that . . . that bag.

> *SARAH comes to her.*

SARAH
Your purse, Mom.

> *STEVEN sings. Maybe TOM joins. KATHLEEN sits.*

ENSEMBLE
Didn't see the lies written in the skies
With the sunshine and promises of rain
My love was in the toil, my tears are in the soil
Oh, these roots are deep, but I no longer hide the pain.

> *KATHLEEN's sitting holding a steering wheel.*

KATHLEEN
Now where did I get to?

SARAH
She's changing but we're still the same.

JOLENE steps into the scene.

JOLENE
No, Mom. There's no church today. It's Wednesday today. Church is on Sunday.

KATHLEEN
But it says Sunday on the calendar.

JOLENE
It says Tuesday too but it's not Tuesday either.

KATHLEEN
Well of course it's not Tuesday. It can't be both Tuesday and Sunday on the same day.

SARAH joins the singing with STEVEN and TOM. SARAH takes over playing.

ENSEMBLE
Just over there is a road that leads to the highway
That'll take me far away, far away
I am standing tall after all I've been through
What's left to do but take the road just over there.

STEVEN is there with KATHLEEN. KATHLEEN is holding a grocery bag, some cash, and a receipt.

STEVEN
Did you get your change, Mom?

KATHLEEN
Uh-huh.

STEVEN
How much change did you get?

> KATHLEEN *looks at him and looks back at the store then back at*
> STEVEN.

This is why you should let me go into the store with you.

KATHLEEN
I'm perfectly capable of going into a store on my own.

STEVEN
Mom. They owe you nine dollars.

KATHLEEN
It's a tip.

STEVEN
You don't tip at a grocery store, Mom.

KATHLEEN
I can tip at a grocery store if I want to. And the young man was very
handsome.

STEVEN
It's Brandon, Mom. Jolene's son.

KATHLEEN
Brandon?

STEVEN
Your grandson?

KATHLEEN
He's so big.

STEVEN
And I'm going to kick his ass for taking your money.

STEVEN joins the singing again. TOM stops playing and is in the kitchen.

ENSEMBLE
Don't know what I feel, if my dreams are real
If these trees are trembling, begging me to stay.
When the north wind blows, the thunder knows
The rain will beat me down, I've already lost my way.

TOM is there with KATHLEEN.

TOM
Thanks for breakfast, Mom.

KATHLEEN
My pleasure, Tommy.

She puts it in front of him.

TOM
Kraft Dinner, Mom? With wieners?

She looks at it for a moment. She recovers.

KATHLEEN
What's wrong with Kraft Dinner and wieners?

TOM
For breakfast, Mom? You don't eat Kraft Dinner and wieners for breakfast.

KATHLEEN
It's just bread and meat. What about fried bologna sandwiches? Same thing. You love that for breakfast.

TOM
Mom.

KATHLEEN
What.

TOM
Djaw forget it was breakfast, Mom?

KATHLEEN
I did not forget / it was breakfast.

TOM
It's okay, / Mom.

KATHLEEN
It's not . . . I'm not . . .

> KATHLEEN *is cut off by the other siblings, who start to sing again.* TOM *joins them.*

ENSEMBLE
Just over there is a road that leads to the highway
That'll take me far away, far away
I am standing tall after all I've been through
What's left to do but take the road just over there.

> *The song ends.*

SARAH
My mom's recent life is playing out before me and it was—

> JOLENE *interrupts with* KATHLEEN *there.*

JOLENE *(to SARAH)*

She ended up downtown with the truck. No idea how she found the keys. We'd been hiding them.

SARAH

Sorry. I took the keys and forgot to put them back.

JOLENE

You gotta keep a better eye on her.

SARAH

She's fine.

JOLENE

Fine? She stopped in the middle of the road. Downtown. Forgot what she was doing there.

SARAH

So? It's not like she held up any traffic.

JOLENE

Tell her what you thought you were doing, Mom.

KATHLEEN

You tell her.

JOLENE

She said she was late for school. Grade five, she said.

KATHLEEN

There ya go.

JOLENE

If you were late for grade five, why were you driving the truck?

KATHLEEN
If you were late and you knew how to drive the truck, you'd take the truck too.

JOLENE
Ten-year-olds don't drive trucks, Mom.

KATHLEEN
We did. We all could drive the truck by the time we were ten.

JOLENE
That's not my point, Mom!

KATHLEEN
You think I'm stopping in the middle of the road just for fun? You think I want to stop in the middle of the road?

Shift. STEVEN *is holding a toothbrush and comb in front of* KATHLEEN.

STEVEN
It's here, Mom. It's here. It's always here. Here's the note to tell you where they are. This note is always on the fridge. And here's the note by your bed to tell you that there's a note on the fridge that tells you what to do in the morning. The toothpaste has a note on it to tell you that this is what you use on your teeth and the toothbrush has a note that says . . . toothbrush. I don't know how many more notes we can put on things.

KATHLEEN
I don't need any more notes. I have Sarah.

STEVEN *looks at* SARAH. *She smiles.*

Sarah bought a waffle iron.

SARAH turns to JOLENE, who has been watching.

SARAH
She recites me poems in the morning while we go for walks.

JOLENE
Poems? She recites poems?

SARAH
What.

JOLENE
She remembers poems?

KATHLEEN
Sometimes.

JOLENE *(to KATHLEEN)*
You remember poems but you . . .

> *She trails off in frustration or from not wanting to hurt her mom.*

KATHLEEN
I what?

JOLENE
You forget . . . all kinds of things. Then you blame us. You get angry /
at us.

KATHLEEN
I don't get / angry. That's—

STEVEN
You yell at us.

KATHLEEN
I never yell at—you yell at me.

JOLENE
We don't yell.

SARAH
They don't. Mostly. It's more like:

JOLENE
No, Mom.

STEVEN
Wrong, Mom.

TOM
They're gone, Mom.

JOLENE
He's dead, Mom.

STEVEN
Not what I said, Mom.

JOLENE
No, Mom.

TOM
Take it slow, Mom.

JOLENE
Are you sure, Mom?

TOM
That's manure, Mom.

JOLENE
We gotta go, Mom.

TOM
It's going to snow, Mom.

STEVEN
You're wearing that, Mom?

JOLENE
You need a hat, Mom.

STEVEN
They sold it, Mom.

TOM
No, hold it, Mom.

STEVEN
Let's *go*.

JOLENE
Mom, *no*!

> *A pause.* KATHLEEN *says nothing but storms out.* TOM *fades off and the other three devolve into a meeting. It's as though they've been sitting there for a bit.*

(partly to us, partly to SARAH*)* Well it's frustrating, you know? And she's not admitting to anything. Why did she call me to start the dishwasher? Isn't that why you're here? Like to start dishwashers and such?

SARAH
What? Start dishwashers?

JOLENE
You know what I mean.

SARAH
She has you on speed dial. And I was out for a walk.

JOLENE looks at SARAH.

And I do not, currently, own a cellphone.

JOLENE *(to us)*
See? Middle of the skating rink. You can't just sit and watch life go by and be satisfied that the earth is still spinning. Sarah seems to think that things will just sort themselves out.

SARAH has noticed that JOLENE just talked to her audience.

JOLENE notices STEVEN sitting there looking at his cellphone.

Steven?

STEVEN
Mmm?

JOLENE
Steven???

He looks up and starts to pay some attention.

STEVEN
Uh . . . yeah. Jolene and I have been doing a lot of thinking.

A little pause. Throughout this next section STEVEN is constantly taking his phone off the table to look at it while JOLENE keeps taking it from his hands and placing it back on the table.

SARAH
Nothing good ever comes after "we've been doing a lot of thinking."

JOLENE
We need to talk about Mom.

SARAH
Is this a meeting?

JOLENE
About Mom.

SARAH
Okay. Good.

JOLENE
Like, we need a strategy.

SARAH
Okay. Great. 'Cause I been sort of watching how / people are—

STEVEN
We're kinda worried about what's going to happen, Sarah.

SARAH
Yeah. Yeah, me too. First, if we could, you know, be a bit more, like, easygoing?

> *JOLENE and STEVEN look at her. They're not sure what she's talking about.*

I mean, I don't think it does any real good to her. You know?

> *Silence.*

Like yelling at her and everything.

JOLENE
We don't yell at her.

SARAH
Well, you know, like being stern, and saying, "No, Mom. That's wrong, Mom," all that.

JOLENE
Mom's still got power of attorney.

SARAH
Um . . . Okay.

JOLENE
She owns the farm.

SARAH
Yeah.

JOLENE
Just her.

SARAH
Right. 'Cause she's the farm owner.

STEVEN
That's true, Sarah, but that's not—

JOLENE
So the supper . . .

She looks to STEVEN *for help. Perhaps she takes his phone and puts it down.*

STEVEN
We were thinking that maybe she'd kind of announce her retirement.
Like officially, you know, so that—

SARAH
Isn't she pretty much—

JOLENE
I don't think you appreciate what could happen if Mom isn't capable of
making decisions about things.

SARAH
What do you mean?

JOLENE
Well, like about the farm and land and stuff.

SARAH
But . . . a supper?

STEVEN
We thought it'd be like a way for us to find out what she wants to do
with the farm.

SARAH
In front of a whole bunch of people?

STEVEN
Maybe take some pressure off.

SARAH
Pressure off? How?

JOLENE
It's a party! It's supposed to be fun.

SARAH
So what's going to happen? You're going to be like, "Gloria, would you mind passing the potato salad? How's everyone doing? Oh, Mom, any idea what you want to do with the farm—you know—before the last marble falls out of your head?"

JOLENE
Wow. That's not—

STEVEN
Okay, if you guys could just—

SARAH
Where's Tom? Where's Tom in all of this? I want to talk to Tom.

> *At that moment* TOM *comes in carrying a plank of wood. No one acknowledges him. He enters and exits a few times during the next exchange, always placing or hammering another plank of wood into something. A sort of makeshift structure is being erected even as the scene is going on around him.*

JOLENE
Tom's busy. He's got the farm to worry about.

SARAH
Well we all have the farm to worry about.

JOLENE
Really. You just said you didn't care.

SARAH
Mom is the farm.

STEVEN
That's very poetic, Sarah, but—

SARAH
Of course I'm worried about the farm.

JOLENE
Really? You been preoccupied with the farm on a daily basis out there in Brampton?

SARAH
Brantford.

JOLENE
Whatever!

STEVEN
Okay. Jolene.

JOLENE
Well come on. I'm talking about on a day-to-day basis.

SARAH
What's Tom saying about all this?

JOLENE
What Tom usually says about it.

STEVEN
Not much.

SARAH
Are you joking me? He's always got an opinion about stuff.

STEVEN
Not about the farm. When it comes to the farm he just shuts up.

JOLENE
He lets his work do the talking.

SARAH
He lets his work—what does that even mean?

STEVEN
Kinda true though.

    JOLENE starts getting ready to go. The musician starts to play.

JOLENE
Anyway, Sarah, we're having the supper. Mom knows and it's Sunday afternoon. I mean we need to get power of attorney and—

SARAH
Who's we?

JOLENE
What?

SARAH
You said "we." Who's we?

    No response.

You and Steven.

JOLENE *(gently)*
Sarah, it makes the most sense.

    SARAH just stands there.

Come on, Steven. Think about it, okay, Sarah? We're not trying to be jerks about this. We just want what's best.

    STEVEN, still more or less on his phone, looks at SARAH as he walks out.

STEVEN
Hey. Uh . . . sorry about this. Really. We're going to be at the bar later if you want to come out for a drink. And, like, if Mom is asleep. I'll beat you at shuffleboard.

SARAH says nothing and watches them go. By the time they're gone a little "fort" structure has been built by TOM. SARAH is with TOM now at his fort.

TOM
Did you go?

SARAH
No. How could I? I was so mad. I woulda gotten drunk and then said some stuff.

TOM
Best time. You can either mean it or apologize later and say you were drunk. It's a win-win.

SARAH watches him work and look around. The music fades out.

SARAH
Took me a half-hour to find you.

TOM
Yeah, that's sort of the idea.

SARAH
I can't believe you still come out here.

TOM
Not very often. A few times in the summer and fall. Then, like, a bunch of times in December and January.

SARAH

You come out here in January?

TOM

Just kidding, bozo. Only an idiot goes anywhere in January.

SARAH

Wow. You been keeping this fort going for like—

TOM

No. No. I forgot all about it. Till like, eight or seven years ago.

SARAH

What. You, like, one day said, "I think I'm gonna go out and work on that old fort. You know, between seeding, combining, haying, I'll just go rebuild the fort—just for kicks."

TOM

I was in the truck just kind of scouting around the spring after Dad died. Seeing how much water we had. I'd grab some soil, see what we were going to plant, watch the hawks. Hawks come way earlier now than they used to. Global warming. Anyway, I went by that little copse of trees and saw the fort. Or, like, what was left of it. And I was just, like, staring at it. The trees looked huge compared to what they were. They'd grown so much that they pulled the planks up with them. And I'm looking at it. And I'm realizing that I'm not going to be able to drive the truck back to the yard and tell Dad what kind of shape things are in and talk about what we should plant and where, and I found myself smiling and crying at the same time. Like grinning really wide but blubbering like a baby. Snot and tears and drool like a fuckin' baby. I mean I built this thing when I was, what? Nine? Ten? It was the best place. Every kid should have a fort. Then when I started getting older, it was a good place to make out with girls. And I had the odd bottle of gin or whatever Dad had kicking around that he wouldn't miss. And he hated gin. So I learned to like gin 'cause he hated it.

SARAH
I love gin.

TOM
Yeah.
(slightly mystical) You take what the provider gives you.

SARAH's looks at him. Pause.

Dad. Dad was the provider.

He chuckles at his own joke.

SARAH
I totally learned to drink out here.

TOM
I know. Mostly though I'd come here to read or smoke pot with my buddies.

Silence. They look around the space. Birds sing. SARAH turns to us.

So, yeah. I was standing there looking at it, and I thought: I should fix this place up and come out here once in a while. So I did. For—I don't know, to remember.

SARAH
People are always telling me I shouldn't live in the past. I live too much in the past.

TOM
People are idiots.

SARAH *(to us)*
There's a couple of things you should probably know about Tom. You okay with that, Tom?

TOM
Meh. Now's as good a time as any.

STEVEN, in shadow, begins to play.

SARAH
So speaking about memory, like I said, Tom's my adopted brother.

TOM
I think they know that.

SARAH
There's Steven, then Jolene, then Tom . . . a few years later. Tom's mom was Indigenous.

TOM
Is, I suppose. She left when I was two or thereabouts. Never knew my dad.

SARAH
We only know the story 'cause Mom told it to us. I mean we were all pretty young and I wasn't even born yet.

TOM
And I was just about to be.

SARAH
So, Mom was a nurse.
She had Steven and Jolene and a few years later went back to work.

*Young KATHLEEN comes forward as a nurse doing something
. . . nurse-like.*

. . . and as Mom tells it, one night at the hospital this woman comes in and she's in labour.

TOM plays his mom—Mary-Jo.

TOM *(as Mary-Jo)*
I'm in labour.

KATHLEEN
All right. Come with me. Do you have a family doctor?

TOM *(as Mary-Jo)*
(No.)

KATHLEEN
What doctor have you been seeing?

TOM *(as Mary-Jo)*
Haven't seen one.

KATHLEEN
Do you know how many weeks you are?

TOM *(as Mary-Jo)*
Not enough.

KATHLEEN
Is there a father?

    Mary-Jo nods.

I mean, is he around? Helping?

    Mary-Jo shakes her head. KATHLEEN *and Mary-Jo go off.*
    Perhaps a little more playing.

SARAH
That night Tom's mom, Mary-Jo, had Tom.

TOM *appears.*

TOM
I was almost seven weeks premature.

Loudly, as much like a newborn as possible.

Waaaaaaaaaa! Waaaaaaaaaa!

SARAH
He had breathing problems and the doctors said he'd be slow.

TOM
Doctors said that a lot about kids like me back then. I was in an incubator for six weeks.

SARAH
Mary-Jo took him home to the reserve, but he'd be back in the hospital every few weeks with something.

Mary-Jo comes in with the baby swaddled.

More often than not my mom was the person she'd see first.

KATHLEEN
How's our little Tommy today then?

TOM *(as Mary-Jo)*
He's sick again, I think.

TOM
Waaaaaaaaaa!!!!

SARAH
This went on for a while and Mom and Tom and Mary-Jo became pretty good friends. And then—as Mom tells it—she just went right up to Dad.

Mary-Jo goes and KATHLEEN *turns to* SARAH, *who is now Robert.*

KATHLEEN
Robert, she's leaving. To Edmonton. She's putting him in foster care.

KATHLEEN *is looking at Robert. He says nothing for a moment.*

SARAH *(as Robert)*
She can't bring him with her?

KATHLEEN
No. She said she can't. She didn't say why. We could foster him.

SARAH *(as Robert)*
Kathleen.

KATHLEEN
One day she might come back for him. That would be okay.

Robert says nothing.

She knows us. She likes us. You used to do work over there. You went to parties and built houses. She knows we're good people. We'd take good care of him.

SARAH *(as Robert)*
Kat.

TOM
And that was it.

SARAH
A few weeks later Tom was at the farm.

TOM
And my mom was gone to Edmonton. Pretty sure, anyway. I've been lookin'.

The slightest of moments.

SARAH *(pleasantly, attempting to lighten the moment)*
So my parents raised him.

TOM
Best non-Indian parents I ever had.

The music has faded out.

SARAH
What do you think should happen to the farm?

TOM
People should keep farming it.

SARAH
Steven and Jolene want the farm.

TOM
I don't think they want the farm.

SARAH
They totally do. They basically told me.

TOM
They don't want the farm, Sarah. They want the land.

SARAH
How do you feel about that?

TOM just shrugs.

Don't you want it?

TOM
I don't want the land. I want the farm. And I don't even want the farm.
I just want the farming.

SARAH
But . . .

TOM
I don't think I'd like running it.

SARAH
You practically run it now.

TOM
I'm just the one who works it. With, like, Mike and Graham like at harvest and stuff. But Jolene runs it. She's been doing the books since even before Mom, like . . . I just go along.

A beat.

Why don't you do it?

SARAH
Me?

TOM
Why not? I'd work for you.

SARAH
You're crazy, Tommy.

TOM
Don't worry about it. Mom'll know what to do with it. And anyway, eventually it's all gonna get swallowed by the big farm next door. Or the even bigger one across the road. Right? I mean look at this place. We're like the farm that time forgot.

Pause.

SARAH
That supper's making me nervous.

TOM
It's making *you* nervous. Just think what it's doing to Mom.

The scene dissolves into KATHLEEN *punching and thrashing at the wind. At the same time this is happening,* SARAH, TOM, *and* STEVEN *have grabbed instruments and there's a bit of a jam going on as* JOLENE *starts to haul food, chairs, and tables for the supper. After a short time the image of* KATHLEEN *fades.*

SARAH *is playing even while she narrates the scene.*

STEVEN
Holy cow, there are a lot of people here!

SARAH
First thing that's out of Steven's mouth when he comes out of the house.

JOLENE *walks on with food or trays or something.*

JOLENE
People are pulling up and looking for places to park. Brandon is enlisted to direct traffic.
(yells) Could use a little help here! Tom? Steven?

TOM
Good thing this is BYOT.

They all look at him.

Bring your own table—ha ha.

STEVEN
People there I haven't seen in years.

Perhaps TOM *breaks away from the jam and begins to help out, carrying things.* SARAH *and* STEVEN *continue.*

SARAH
Like Gary and Shelley. Dog breeders. We got all our dogs from them. They're always smiling and happy. Kinda like "How's it goin'?"

STEVEN
No, it's more like this: "How's it goin'? All ready for the big supper?"

JOLENE
Yeah, and Shelley's like, "We brought my famous ham!"

KATHLEEN *appears.*

KATHLEEN
Never heard of it. Can't be that famous.

SARAH
And Mom, who disappeared up the field for a few hours, is back and a particular kind of cranky.

TOM *(as Rick Rivera)*
Hallo! We're happy to be at your party! We hab so much foods!

Now perhaps STEVEN *breaks away and puts down his instrument.* SARAH *continues.*

SARAH
There's Rick Rivera, the Filipino man with his wife and five kids.

KATHLEEN
Oh dear God, those kids scream like they're on fire.

STEVEN
Oh yeah, there's Hans Weber, the farmer a couple of farms over who's been in Canada fifty-three years and still has the biggest German accent you ever—

SARAH *(as Hans Weber)*
Hi. I have sausage for Kathleen?

JOLENE
There's Al and Deb.

STEVEN *(as Al)*
I brought Deb. She's delicious!

JOLENE *(as Deb)*
Oh, Alan, stop.

STEVEN *(as Al)*
You are! All plump and juicy.

> *Deb looks at him. Pause.*

So . . . uh . . . salad? Salad good?

> *The siblings are starting to have fun with this.*

SARAH
There's the Brooks brothers.

> *TOM steps up.*

TOM *(as first Brooks brother)*
Hi.

There's a moment where everyone looks at each other—not sure who the other Brooks brother is. SARAH *stops playing.* TOM *becomes the other brother.*

TOM *(as second Brooks brother)*
Hey.

Slight pause. Music resumes. Maybe TOM *playing now.*

JOLENE
Bob, that artist who makes those sculptures out of old bicycles.

STEVEN *(as Bob)*
Hey, I brought a curry.

KATHLEEN
Great. Now I'll have the shits for three days.

SARAH
Wendy and her husband, Bart. Wendy's always saying things like:

(as Wendy) "We brought a turkey. Other than Bart here!"

KATHLEEN
Him I like. She's a bag of wind.

STEVEN
Oh. There's the pottery woman.

TOM *(as Pottery Woman)*
Rhonda, honey. I brought desserts. Gluten-free, no sugar.

KATHLEEN
Hard to call it dessert.

TOM and STEVEN move somewhere with their arms raised over their heads.

TOM
More tables!

STEVEN
And more comin'!

JOLENE
Over there, please. Oh, and grab the two things of potato salad and put one of them at one end and one at the other.

SARAH
There must be a dozen tables lined up together in an L shape.

TOM
Where d'you want this potato salad?

JOLENE
Anywhere, Tom, but we still need pickles.

TOM
Pickles.

STEVEN
Brandon's using a lightsaber to guide traffic. Hope that's okay.

SARAH
To say the whole town was there is a bit of an exaggeration.

JOLENE
But really, it would be easier to count the number of people who weren't here.

SARAH
There were even a bunch of guys from Tom's hockey team. There was Gus. Who for some reason everyone called Gussy. 'Cause that's shorter.

STEVEN *(as Gus)*
Not shorter. Just uhhh funner.

SARAH
Jeff 1.

TOM *(as Jeff 1)*
Hey.

SARAH
And Jeff 2.

> *Again, they're not sure who should take on Jeff 2, so* TOM *takes on both.*

TOM *(as Jeff 2)*
Hey.

> *The music fades.*

JOLENE
And everybody's tellin' stories or sharin' gossip and passing food. Like Mike.

STEVEN *(as Mike)*
Okay. So.

SARAH
Just a warning. Don't ever get Mike tellin' a story. I don't care how badly you need something explained.

JOLENE
Even if aliens come to your farm and carve out half a dozen crop circles in your wheat, get drunk over a campfire singing Dwight Yoakam songs, and, just for kicks, anal probe everyone down at the bar.

SARAH
And Mike is the ONLY witness to it all. DO NOT ask Mike to tell you the story.

STEVEN *(as Mike, to everyone)*
Okay. So.

SARAH/JOLENE
Here we go.

STEVEN *(as Mike)*
Oh man. Crazy story I got for ya. Crazy. You're not gonna believe this. It was—I'm gonna say it was a transcendent experience. Really.

JOLENE
Really.

STEVEN *(as Mike)*
Yeah.

JOLENE
Transcendent.

STEVEN *(as Mike)*
Oh yeah. Like I've had transcendent experiences before, like? And each one is of a particular, you know, nature. And this one doesn't seem so strange unless you—what you call it these days? Unpack it, you know?

JOLENE
Unpack it.

STEVEN *(as Mike)*
Yeah. Like take it apart. See what it's all about, you know? What it means and all that.

JOLENE
Who's got the pickles? Any pickles down at that end?

Pause.

Well? If you're gonna tell it . . .

STEVEN *(as Mike)*
Right. Okay. Uh . . . I could use some more of that turkey. But I can't have turkey without cranberries. So if . . . if anyone . . .

He looks down the table and waits. Maybe someone passes him something, maybe not.

Okay, so I'm haulin' these saplings—these *(makes air quotes)* "aspens" in the back of my—

SARAH
So they weren't necessarily aspens?

STEVEN *(as Mike)*
Huh?

JOLENE
Well you just air-quoted.

STEVEN *(as Mike)*
Huh?

SARAH
You air-quoted aspens.

STEVEN *(as Mike)*
Yeah. I know. That's 'cause Kathleen specifically asked me to go buy some aspens. Not poplars. Not balsams. Aspens.

JOLENE
Gotcha.

STEVEN *(as Mike)*
Aspens. Trembling aspens. That's what Kathleen calls them.

JOLENE
Okay then. Trembling aspens.

STEVEN *(as Mike)*
Yeah. Saplings—

SARAH
What'd you need them for?

JOLENE
Pass the ham.

STEVEN *(as Mike)*
That's not the point.

SARAH
I know that's not the point, I'm just askin'.

STEVEN *(as Mike)*
Kathleen wants them. So I'm drivin' along in my truck with—

JOLENE
What's Mom want with a truckful of aspen saplings?

STEVEN *(as Mike)*
She wants me to plant—or *she* wants to plant but I'll prob'ly do it—
some aspens along the lane. She says the lane doesn't have enough
trees. Or some have kinda, you know, fallen apart—

JOLENE *(to us)*
A bunch cracked in half in that storm last year.

STEVEN *(as Mike)*
So, like I said, there I am in my truck just—

SARAH
Wait. Where's Mom?

JOLENE
She was here a minute ago.

> *Everyone stops and looks around. There's a moment of frozen
> silence.*

SARAH
Steven. Entertain people. We gotta go find Mom.

STEVEN *(looks around awkwardly)*
How 'bout that ham, huh?

> *SARAH drifts to the piano.*

> *Shift to KATHLEEN, standing alone in the yard staring up into
> the sky. Her eyes drift back and forth and her body sways with
> her eyes, as though she is the one in the sky swaying back and
> forth like a kite.*

KATHLEEN
I like your kite, Doris.

JOLENE steps in and becomes Doris—childhood friend of KATHLEEN's. They're about eight.

JOLENE *(as Doris)*
My dad made it. He makes kites like my mom makes soup. Just throws some stuff together and in a minute it's up in the air flying. It doesn't matter what it's made of. It flies. If he had more string, I'm pretty sure it would go into the clouds.

KATHLEEN continues to look up.

KATHLEEN
It has so many colours.

JOLENE *(as Doris)*
I know. My dad found all this old paper? And then gathered these pieces of um dowelling that he found? He uses this special glue. He says the glue's really light. It's a special glue. He makes the glue.

KATHLEEN
Your dad makes glue?

JOLENE *(as Doris)*
My dad can make anything. He made the tail out of pieces of cloth from some curtains. Don't tell my mom.

KATHLEEN
Don't tell your mom what?

JOLENE *(as Doris)*
I don't know. About the curtains.

More music. KATHLEEN looking up.

Do you want to fly it?

KATHLEEN
Yes, please.

> *Doris comes over and hands* KATHLEEN *the string. Carefully* KATHLEEN *takes it. She flies the kite, swaying back and forth with it. She smiles, giggles.*

It flies really well.

> *Landon (played by* TOM*) comes over. He's nine. He's got an airplane made of light wood that you can throw in the air like a glider.*

TOM *(as Landon)*
Like my plane, Kathleen?

> KATHLEEN *glances at it. She nods and looks back to the kite.*

KATHLEEN
Yes.

TOM *(as Landon)*
That's our kite.

KATHLEEN
Doris said I could fly it.

> *They watch her fly it. Landon is bored.*

TOM *(as Landon)*
I bought it. I bought it with money I saved.

KATHLEEN
You bought what?

TOM *(as Landon)*
This plane.

KATHLEEN
How did you save the money?

SARAH gets up from the piano and steps forward.

SARAH
And then, just behind the barn, I see her. But Tom and Jolene are already there.

KATHLEEN
I said how did you save the money?

TOM is no longer Landon.

TOM *(slowly turning back into TOM)*
How did I save what money?

KATHLEEN stares at TOM.

Mom?

KATHLEEN
Whose . . . whose kite is this?

She turns to JOLENE.

Where did you get that dress, Doris?

JOLENE
What?

KATHLEEN
You're not Doris.

JOLENE
Mom? You okay?

KATHLEEN
What?

Then, realizing where she is and what's she's doing, KATHLEEN *looks up and lets the kite go, watching it disappear.*

JOLENE
Mom? What are you staring at?

KATHLEEN
I was . . . I was—where is that plane going to, do you think? With the
. . . the white stream trailing behind it. Where do you think that would
be going?

TOM *(not really interested)*
I don't know. Edmonton? I don't know.

KATHLEEN
Edmonton.

There's a pause, a moment, and then KATHLEEN *quietly walks away with them and the supper scene resumes as people sit back down.*

SARAH
It's like time has frozen. We sit back down at the supper.

As they all sit back down, Mike kicks back into his story.

STEVEN *(as Mike)*
Everything okay?

SARAH
Oh yeah. Great.

JOLENE
Can I get you anything, Mom? Can we get Mom a plate of something?

KATHLEEN
Who has the potatoes?

JOLENE
Let's get some potatoes for Mom. Potatoes? Now, what were we talking about?

STEVEN *(as Mike)*
I was tellin' my story, but I can stop if you—

JOLENE
No. No. Go ahead. Tell it.

STEVEN *(as Mike)*
No, it's okay. Really, I don't gotta—

JOLENE
No. Mike. Tell it. Now. Trembling poplars and—

STEVEN *(as Mike)*
Aspens, actually.

JOLENE
Aspens, right. Go ahead. Sounds like a great story, huh, Mom?

KATHLEEN
Can't wait.

SARAH *(to us)*
Something's changed. In Mom.

JOLENE
Potatoes?

STEVEN *(as Mike)*
So I place an order for some aspens. Like I said, trembling aspens.

SARAH
So now our little garden centre carries aspen saplings?

STEVEN *(as Mike)*
Roy brought 'em in special for me.

JOLENE
Wow. Look at Roy showing some initiative. Hey, Mom?

KATHLEEN
What?

STEVEN *(as Mike)*
Annnnyyyyyywaaaaaays! I'm drivin' along the lane with the saplings and I see something up a ways in the middle of the road, and it's a good size and it's not movin'.

KATHLEEN
Can I get some turkey?

JOLENE
Turkey? Anyone seen—

STEVEN *(as Mike)*
And I think it must be a dog but it's not one of yours. Like it's not Toby and it's not Biscuit.

SARAH
Biscuit wouldn't be out on the road anyway.

KATHLEEN
Stuffing. I want stuffing.

STEVEN *(as Mike)*
And then I think it's a coyote.

KATHLEEN
Goddamn coyotes.

STEVEN *(as Mike)*
But I get closer and it's not a coyote either.

KATHLEEN
Can someone pass me the turkey? And stuffing?

JOLENE
Has no one found the—

STEVEN *(as Mike)*
Guess what it was?

JOLENE
Mike, can we—

SARAH
What?

STEVEN *(as Mike)*
Guess.

JOLENE
Oh for shit's sake.

Something is handed to JOLENE.

Thank you! Mom! Here's the turkey.

SARAH
Badger.

STEVEN *(as Mike)*
Nope.

KATHLEEN
Who do you gotta kill around here to get—

JOLENE
Potatoes, Mom. I know. Potatoes. Tom? Can you see if— Where's Tom?

SARAH
Turkey!

STEVEN *(as Mike)*
Turkey?

SARAH
Yeah, like a wild—

JOLENE
A goat.

SARAH
We don't have goats.

JOLENE
Maybe it's an escaped goat. Right, Mom?

STEVEN *(as Mike)*
From where?

KATHLEEN
Anything resembling a vegetable? Coleslaw even?

JOLENE
Vegetables? Got any guesses what it was, Mom?

SARAH
Bear?

STEVEN *(as Mike)*
Nope.

JOLENE
We give up, Mike. Any vege—

KATHLEEN
Just pull something green out of the ground for heaven's sake!

JOLENE
Here's the potatoes you wanted. I'll find you some vegetables. Mike, we need you to—

KATHLEEN
Who's running this "feast" anyway?

SARAH
Bear cub.

JOLENE
Sarah, can you—

JOLENE is putting potatoes down in front of KATHLEEN.

STEVEN *(as Mike)*
Not a bear, not a cub, not a badger, not a—

JOLENE
Mike, can you finish the—

KATHLEEN

Fox! It was a fox! It was the fox, all right?? The same fox that showed up when Tom first came to the farm. Goddammit! I told you I hate goddamn scalloped potatoes!

Everything stops. Including the music. Everyone looks at her.
A moment of dead silence. Then TOM, *in the shadows, begins*
to play.

JOLENE *(quietly)*

No, of course you don't like scalloped potatoes, Mom. I forgot. Any baked potatoes around?

Quickly, STEVEN *comes and gives her another plate and a baked*
potato.

STEVEN

Here ya go, Mom.

KATHLEEN

And coyotes'll get that fox the first chance they get. Now, where's the rest of my food? Who. Took. The. Rest. Of. My. Food?

JOLENE

Mom, I don't think you had anything but—

KATHLEEN

I had some potato salad and some pickled asparagus! And you took that too!

JOLENE

Okay, Mom. Okay. It's okay, Mom.

KATHLEEN

You trying to starve me? I didn't even have my ham! Whatshername's famous ham!

SARAH
And Jolene is trying to hush Mom.

JOLENE
Shh, Mom. Shh. It's okay.

SARAH
Which Mom hates.

JOLENE *(through her teeth, partly)*
Well most of the time she quiets down.

SARAH
And people are gazing at their food like scolded school kids.

Silence.

STEVEN *(as Mike)*
Anyways, yeah, it was a fox. Just sitting in the middle of the road. Just lookin' up at me. It never moves. Doesn't care if I'm there or not.

KATHLEEN just stares at her plate. She slowly starts to take a mouthful of food. Everyone watches. She chews. Silence. She looks up.

KATHLEEN *(challenging them)*
What's everybody staring at? Play on! Play on, I say! More wine!

Speeches! Who's going to go first? Who wants to declare their undying admiration for their darling mother? Jolene? As the one who came up with this . . . this . . . party. You probably have something to say?

JOLENE
No, that's . . . that's okay. I don't need to—

Very slowly JOLENE *stands up.* TOM, *who has disappeared, begins to pick quietly in the darkness.*

KATHLEEN
No. I insist. Please tell us all how much you love your dear ma.

They all stare at each other.

JOLENE *(to us)*
All I had planned to do is make a toast. A toast! That's it! This whole speech thing is a bad idea—Sarah was right. And so I stand there talkin' about what a great day this is and how . . . great . . . everyone is for coming and how . . . uh . . . great Mom is and how Mom and I have always been really close—which is a lie—and I just start rambling and rambl—

> KATHLEEN *interrupts* JOLENE *and claps sarcastically.*

KATHLEEN
Bravo! Bravo! What a performance!
(with a mouth full of food) Anyone else? Steven? You wanna be Mom's favourite?

> STEVEN *stands up. Again, slowly.*

STEVEN *(to us)*
I have no idea what I'm actually saying. I'm a little drunk and suddenly nervous and so I start talking with my hands a lot and saying "uh" a lot, and asking people if they have enough food and more "uhhs" and I think I say something about my love for Mom and and . . . and for the farm, I think, and uhh, for everybody and I'm not sure but I think I just drift off and sit back . . .

> STEVEN *drifts off and sits back down.*

KATHLEEN
Where's Tom? Where'd Tom get to? Tom not going to give a speech? I bet he'd have a lot to say.
(calling out) Wouldn't you, Tom?

SARAH *(to us)*
But Tom's not there. He got out while the getting was—

> *The lights shift to where* TOM *is playing the guitar, looking casually out at us.*

TOM *(to us)*
I'm not stupid. I could feel things piling up as the supper went on. I get the hell outta there and head down to the bar. It's not open mic night, but when there's nobody around—like a Sunday night—I go, "Hey, Rick, can we make it an open mic night?" And he always goes, "Knock yourself out, Tommy." So I play. To like three people. Including Rick. And in between my two fifteen-minute sets I play some pool. 'Member when you could smoke in the bar? Nothin' like shootin' pool with a cigarette hangin' from the corner of your mouth and you time your beer drinkin' with your pool shots. And that feelin' you get when you're playin' the best pool of your life till about the start of the fourth beer and then the angles get bad and the ones you sunk in the first coupla games seem almost impossible all of a sudden. I miss that. And my second set is always interesting too. What were we talkin' about again? Oh yeah. The supper. So I leave the supper and head down to the bar. Didn't think anybody would notice. I may have had other reasons. But we won't get into that here.

> *Lighting change.* TOM *plays again. We're back at the supper.*
> KATHLEEN *is standing, looking out at people.*

KATHLEEN
I have something to say.

KATHLEEN sits there for a moment. KATHLEEN stands up, slowly, as SARAH narrates.

SARAH
And she stands there, and her mind's probably miles away, flying a kite somewhere, and she tells us about aspens in the fall, hawks in the spring, and why the story about the fox makes perfect sense to her. And then she tells us who's getting the farm. And we all sit there not knowing what to say.

JOLENE
And it's Sarah's farm, Sarah's land, Sarah's power of attorney, Sarah's . . .

Incredulity—a pause.

Sarah's.

TOM
Told ya.

Silence. TOM's guitar stops.

End of Act I.

ACT II

TOM begins to play/pick a waltz on the guitar. After a time,
SARAH appears. She is sitting centre with skates.

SARAH *(to us)*
When I was a kid and sat in the middle of the rink, I wasn't just sitting there. I was doing things. I was watching people. Back then on a Sunday afternoon so many people from the town would be there. I'd watch and imagine who they were, what their lives were like. I'd give them names, jobs, even what kinds of pets they had. Or I'd pretend I knew what they were thinking as they skated around and around. I didn't want to skate around and around with no place to go. It made me scared. I wanted to be somewhere. Solid and firm. Ice is . . . slippery. You don't know what's going to happen.

And sitting there, I would sing songs to myself or recite poetry. My mom knew so many poems. She would always tell me a poem to put me to bed.

KATHLEEN appears as her younger self and goes to SARAH as
though she is reciting a bedtime story.

KATHLEEN
The wind, it comes at night,
Trying to claw the house apart . . .

SARAH
This was my favourite poem of all. It terrified me. I thought the wind was a person.

KATHLEEN
It goes at all the windows.
The windows shudder in their frames.

SARAH
I saw the wind's fingers. I thought they would pluck me out of my bed
and carry me away.

> *Now* SARAH *begins to echo the poem with* KATHLEEN *as though
> she knows parts of it.*

SARAH/KATHLEEN
The wind wants you to come out and be blown . . .

KATHLEEN
Forever . . .

SARAH
Forever . . .

KATHLEEN
Through a world . . .

SARAH/KATHLEEN
Moving too fast for you to see it.

KATHLEEN
The way the wind sees it.
So what if you lie under your covers . . .

SARAH
And shiver . . .

KATHLEEN
That same wind goes through your lungs.
Through and through . . .

KATHLEEN *drifts away and is gone.*

SARAH/KATHLEEN
Through and through . . .

SARAH
Through and through and . . .

We're back at the rink. KATHLEEN's *gone.*

. . . and around and around and around and around . . .

The following Sunday I take Mom's old skates and head to the rink. It's a bit run down and there are fewer people than I remember. For a while I skate along with everyone else until I realize that I was terrible at skating because I'd never really learned. I was always sitting in the middle of the ice. So that's what I do. I sit down in the middle of the ice. People laugh. A few remember.

STEVEN *appears skating around her.*

STEVEN *(as Hans Weber)*
Ah! Sarah. Just like ze old days, huh? You sitting in ze ice again!
(laughs)

SARAH
But I liked watching the world go by. And people who'd been at the supper skate by and ask how Mom was. Like Shelley and her husband.

JOLENE *(as Shelley)*
Your Mom okay? Sorry 'bout what happened, eh?

SARAH
And then she and Gary skate away arm in arm like Olympians.

The music has ended. SARAH *is taking her skates off.*

A week later and Steven's back in Calgary and Jolene . . . doesn't come around. At all. It's just me and Mom at the farmhouse. Harvest is long done and Tom's getting things ready for winter, cleaning, oiling, changing, hunkering down—

> TOM *walks through with a large box of clothes, singing snippets of words from the song "Close To You."*

> *He stops in front of* SARAH.

TOM
. . . She's dancing to records in the parlour.

SARAH *(to us)*
Suddenly, old songs that I heard as a kid are filling the house again. *(to* TOM*)* What's with the box?

TOM
Oh. Bunch of dad's old clothes. She wants me to clean out the attic. Not sure what to do with 'em.

SARAH
Sally Ann?

TOM
Yep. I guess. Nice suit in here. I'll put the stuff in the barn for now.

SARAH
The barn? Clothes? That people will wear?

TOM
Okay. My place.

> *He exits with the box.*

SARAH
But Mom's just getting going. She's out in the field, cooking in the kitchen . . .

> KATHLEEN *appears. She's in a housecoat but with a hat and purse. The music stops abruptly.*

Mom?

KATHLEEN
Time for church.

SARAH
It's Wednesday.

> KATHLEEN *says nothing. Just stands there. Expectantly.*

There's no church on Wednesdays, Mom.

> *Pause.*

Sunday is when church is. I'll take you to church on Sunday.

> KATHLEEN *slowly walks off as* SARAH *talks to us.*

When Mom's rested, she's fine. We look at old photo albums and listen to records and even read poetry together, but when she's tired—

> KATHLEEN *is there again wearing some different accessories to suggest a different day but otherwise it's identical to the previous moment.*

It's Thursday. There's no church on Thursday. Sunday we go to church. You wanted to look for the fox today.

KATHLEEN
The fox.

SARAH
You wanted to go look for it.

> *Pause.* KATHLEEN *thinks on this and walks away.*

I'm trying to keep normal and calm but she wants to go in five different directions at once. I mean, Jolene said routine is—

> KATHLEEN *is there again. Different hat, scarf, purse perhaps. She's ready for church.*

It's only Friday, Mom. Friday's when we go do a little shopping and run some errands.

> KATHLEEN *doesn't walk away this time but only changes a hat or purse right in front of* SARAH.

It's Saturday, Mom. Tomorrow. Tomorrow. Sunday.

> KATHLEEN *walks away slowly—a bit lost, puzzled.*

> TOM *is there wiping down a machine part.* SARAH *looks or goes to him.*

TOM
She's a busy woman.

SARAH
. . . And she has a daily hairdresser schedule too! 'Cept I can't keep up.

TOM
You can't keep up? With what? It's just her dreams.

SARAH
With saying no all the time! I feel like Jolene.

TOM
Jolene probably felt like you.

SARAH
That's not fair. Mom's way worse now.

TOM
And don't forget the two jobs that Jolene has. Not including the farm books.

He's gone. Busy doing something else.

KATHLEEN appears somewhere else, gardening and talking to herself.

SARAH turns to her and then to us.

KATHLEEN
Marigolds.

SARAH
And then she's gardening.

KATHLEEN
And begonias.

SARAH
In the driveway. In November. In a housecoat. Two inches of snow and she's scooping it up and planting imaginary seeds and covering them with snow. Over and over in the same—

KATHLEEN is somewhere else.

KATHLEEN *(quietly responding to her children)*
Okay, Steven. But be careful!

> *SARAH stays firmly in the "real" world.* KATHLEEN *is audible, but barely.*

SARAH
That's snow, Mom!

KATHLEEN
Jo. You can't be bringing baby animals back to the house. That bird is someone's baby.

SARAH
Mom. Come in. Look at your knees!

KATHLEEN
I'd rather you climb the other tree, Steven. Just climb the / other tree.

SARAH
Mom, you're not dressed—

KATHLEEN
Jolene, put that back. You don't know where the mom is.

SARAH
Mom. Come in. Don't make me / have to drag you in here, Mom.

KATHLEEN
You're stealing that baby from someone.

SARAH
What? Stealing what baby? What are you—

KATHLEEN
You put that baby back right—

Where's Tommy?

SARAH *(in present)*
In the barn, I think. He's just putting— Mom. Mom, come in the house!

KATHLEEN
Steven, that tree's too—

> *Then* KATHLEEN *drifts away calling.*

Tommy! Tom, where'd you get to? Tommy?

SARAH *(in present)*
No, Mom! It's not time to be—

> *The scene with* KATHLEEN *is gone and* SARAH *is back talking to* TOM.

TOM
She's not looking for me, the man. She's looking for me, the boy.

SARAH
Why, though?

> TOM *shrugs.*

I can't keep up with her. I'm not sure what to do. If she doesn't nap, she's all out of sorts and I spend the afternoon trying to keep her from—she keeps looking for a hill.

TOM
A hill?

SARAH
And she's out to the field every day and yells at . . . the sky, the geese . . . Dad. You.

TOM
Me?

SARAH
I don't know, she says your name. She talks to Dad. By the time I get there, she's tired out and quiet.

TOM
Every day?

SARAH
Every day.

TOM *(tiny pause)*
Leave her be.

SARAH
Leave her be? She goes out in her housecoat. It was minus eighty or something last night.

TOM
It was minus twelve, for shit's sake. God, prairie people move away and forget they ever saw winter in their lives.

SARAH
Well it's fuckin' cold.

TOM
It's winter.

SARAH
It's November. It's fall!

TOM
Move to Mexico, ya turd!

SARAH *(breathes)*
Okay. Look. I just need a night. Okay? I just . . . I just want to go to the
bar for a bit and hang out, okay? Just get away from things for a night.
Can you stay with her?

TOM
Nope.

SARAH
What? No??

TOM
Got plans.

SARAH
Plans? What kind of plans?

TOM
Goin' to the bar.

SARAH doesn't know what to say. She starts to walk away.

Take her to church.

SARAH
I do. Every Sunday, and / I hate church.

TOM
No. When she wants to go.

SARAH
That's like every day.

TOM *(so?)*
You got some pressing affairs we don't know about?

SARAH
What?

TOM
You some international jet-setter?

SARAH
What the fuck—

TOM
Just stop whining about it, for shit's sake.

He starts to walk away. SARAH *turns to us.*

SARAH
And then he just turns and / walks away . . .

TOM *(to us, cutting her off)*
Then he turns and walks away, leaving her blah blah blah.

A pause. SARAH *is speechless. He looks back at her.*

Well, I don't see the point of narrating the obvious. I think they can figure it out.

SARAH *just stands there for a moment.*

KATHLEEN *appears, dressed for church.*

KATHLEEN
Church, please.

SARAH *sighs and drops her shoulders.*

Fine!

SARAH grabs two chairs and angrily puts together a car for them. They get in. SARAH slams the door.

They drive in silence. One angry, the other . . . not. They get there. SARAH is steaming.

SARAH
There. Church.

KATHLEEN *(looking)*
Oh.

SARAH
That's right, Mom. It's closed.

KATHLEEN
Oh.

SARAH
That's right. There's no church today. You see? Nobody's here!

KATHLEEN *(thinks for a moment)*
Then why did we come?

SARAH
Why did we come?? Because you wanted to.

But she stops herself and thinks.

You wanted to.

A moment as they sit there looking out.

All you want to do is fly a kite and we keep holding it down.

Should we come back tomorrow?

KATHLEEN
Come back where?

SARAH
To church.

KATHLEEN
I don't know.

> *After a moment* STEVEN *starts to play. They sit in silence for a time before* SARAH *starts to sing as* KATHLEEN *stares out, waiting.*

I'LL FOLLOW

SARAH *(singing)*
You seem to listen like angels are singing
Secrets whispered, church bells ringing
But all I hear is the wind.

You travel to places I don't understand
Searching through time for a safe place to land
And I'm still here in the wind.

> SARAH *mimes driving away. She puts the car in gear and* KATHLEEN *looks out at passing things.*

Oh, promises made
No, don't be afraid
Don't be afraid 'cause I'm always behind you
Trust in the moment and know love will guide you
I'll follow if you lead the way.

> *They get out of the car,* SARAH *moving the chairs away as* KATHLEEN *drifts off. The music continues.*

(to us) We go to church every day until . . . there's church. I start doing whatever she asks. To Misty's to get her hair done, two, three times a week.

> *SARAH grabs a guitar. She joins STEVEN playing, who perhaps eventually stops or trails off.*

She sits in the second chair and Misty cuts the air around her head.

> *TOM steps up and becomes Misty and mimes chatting up KATHLEEN, who listens and smiles and says nothing.*

Or we head to Billy's for a tune-up. Bill just goes along. I mean he sees that car every fifteen klicks or so, but he doesn't mind. Nobody seems to mind.

> *TOM plays Bill. He's wiping his hands on a rag and hands KATHLEEN her keys. Happily she walks away, smiling at SARAH.*

Around town she's going up to people we barely know and chatting.

> *KATHLEEN steps down stage and looks to the audience.*

KATHLEEN
Have you seen the hill? The hill where the fox goes?

> *KATHLEEN looks out for a moment as though listening and then ambles away off stage.*

SARAH *(singing)*
Oh, through a world that is moving too fast
You're fighting your way to a place in the past
Breaks my heart open wide . . .

> *Moments later KATHLEEN re-enters with a couple of picture frames and proceeds to examine them and then look to walls*

as though deciding where to place them. This happens with the following verses:

. . . The only thing that I can do when you leave
Is hope you'll come back, although time will deceive
But I'll be here by your side

Oh, promises made
No, don't be afraid
Don't be afraid 'cause I'm always behind you
Trust in the moment and know love will guide you
I'll follow if you lead the way.

And at home we're moving the piano back and forth, putting up pictures, taking them down . . .

> KATHLEEN *is busy moving picture frames and then . . .*

And whoever she decides I am, that's who I am.

> *. . . comes in with a tray of sandwiches.*

KATHLEEN
Peggy, I'll just take these sandwiches out to the boys.

SARAH
Okay, Kathleen.

> SARAH *watches her mom exit. During the next verse* KATHLEEN *re-enters and comes to centre immediately in front of* SARAH *and gets on her hands and knees, gardening.*

(singing) Sometimes in life we forget where we're going
We lose our path without ever knowing
We cling to each moment, we try to remember
But memories fall like the leaves in September

I'll follow if you lead the way
I'll follow if you lead the way.

The way our farm is laid out, you can see the road that leads directly to the driveway from a long way. It runs along the treeline where the aspens are, along the front quarter and right in front of the farmhouse and the barn. You can watch a car come along that road for days.

She turns back to her mom.

We should go back to the house, Mom.

KATHLEEN stands there and watches, and then, seeing who it is, smiles and waves.

KATHLEEN is gone and suddenly JOLENE and STEVEN are there in the kitchen with SARAH.

(to us) They're sayin' Mom knew all along.

JOLENE
Well she did.

SARAH *(to us)*
They think Mom and I had a plan.

JOLENE
I think you did.

SARAH
It's nice to see you too, Steven. You come from Calgary just for this?

STEVEN
Well, I hadn't planned on it, but Jolene said it'd be important if we all—

JOLENE *(to SARAH)*
That's why you came back.

SARAH
They think Mom and me were "in cahoots."

STEVEN
I was just making a joke.

SARAH
Ha ha. Some joke.

STEVEN
So I came up with "cahoots."

SARAH
You didn't come up with "cahoots." It's already a word.

JOLENE *(to us)*
It's their own little conspiracy's what I think.

SARAH
They're sayin' that Mom called me in Ontario and told me to come back just for the supper.

JOLENE
She never wanted me to have the farm anyway.

SARAH
What are you / talking about?

JOLENE
But you never worked on the farm for one minute.

SARAH
Not true.

JOLENE
Never cared about the farm.

SARAH
Not true.

JOLENE
Never wanted the farm.

SARAH
True.

JOLENE
When we were teenagers, we'd work on the farm all the time while you would lay around in that fort Tom made.

SARAH
Also true.

STEVEN *(to JOLENE)*
Uh . . . that was mostly you and Tom.

JOLENE
Well you worked the farm / sometimes.

STEVEN
And Sarah was too young to—

JOLENE
Steven. You're not helping!

SARAH
So. Mom called me and told me all about the will and that I was going to get the farm and to hurry back.

JOLENE
Well it sort of—

SARAH
And that made me leave Chris?

JOLENE
I still don't know why you left Chris.

SARAH
You want to hear a theory? I think Mom had no idea what she was going to do and was more and more scared and confused with people asking questions and kids running around and I think she got angry when you gave her scalloped potatoes and retaliated.

JOLENE
That's your theory.

SARAH
That's my theory.

JOLENE
Your scalloped potato theory.

SARAH
My scalloped potato theory.

STEVEN (*fake mysteriously*)
Ahh. The scalloped potato theory.

JOLENE
Steven. Shut up.

STEVEN
What the—

JOLENE *(back to* SARAH*)*
Then how do you explain the will? It's not just what she said. You have
power of attorney, you have the farm, you have it all, just like that, and
you think this is about scalloped potatoes?

SARAH
It's not about scalloped potatoes. It's about not paying attention.

JOLENE
To what?

SARAH
To Mom!

JOLENE
Yeah, you parading her around town, showing her off.

SARAH
Showing her / off? Are you insane?

JOLENE
You've got the whole town believing that you're the rightful heir to the
family farm. That this was the plan all along.

SARAH
Does this look like any kind of plan?

STEVEN
Jolene thinks you're trying to make it look charming.

SARAH
Charming.

STEVEN
Quaint.

SARAH
You come up with that word too?

STEVEN
Ha ha. Very funny.

SARAH
I don't have time for this. It'll be church time soon.

JOLENE
It's Thursday.

SARAH
I know what day it is. And then she'll be going for her hair appointment.

JOLENE
How many / hair appointments does—?

SARAH grabs a tray of sandwiches and offers one to JOLENE and STEVEN.

SARAH
Oh. Sandwich anyone?

JOLENE
No thanks—

She looks at them.

What's in them?

SARAH
Nothing.

STEVEN *(with a mouth full)*
Butter.

SARAH
Mom makes them for farm lunches.

JOLENE
Farm lunches? For who?

STEVEN has eaten one and is on his next one.

STEVEN
Oh man, white bread and butter sandwiches. The best.

JOLENE
She's made forty sandwiches!

SARAH
And stew.

JOLENE
And stew!

SARAH
For, like, Dad and the boys, she says.

JOLENE
There's nothing in the sandwiches! And there's nobody to eat them.

SARAH
It's only some bread. I'll make grill cheeses. The stew's good. I supervised.

JOLENE
You're missing the point.

SARAH
No, you're missing the point. I'm trying / to show you what Mom . . .

JOLENE
I don't think you're good for her.

SARAH
What?

JOLENE
You heard me.

SARAH
How am I not good for her?

JOLENE
I don't think you should be living with her right now.

SARAH
Oh? Who's going to take care of her. You? You gonna take some leave from your job and just hole up here every day? Help Tom with the combining?

JOLENE
Wouldn't be the first time.

SARAH
You need me here. Mom needs me here.

JOLENE
Doesn't Chris need you?

SARAH
What does Chris have to do with this?

JOLENE
When are you planning on going back?

SARAH
What if I'm not going back?

JOLENE
You can't stay here.

SARAH
Who says?

JOLENE
We were doing fine. We had things under control.

SARAH
No, you didn't. You never saw your family. You don't speak to your—
Roy. The only time I've seen him was at the supper and then he was
mostly chatting with Tom and the boys and kicking tractor tires. He
barely said hello to me.

It's JOLENE's turn to get quiet.

Jolene?

JOLENE turns to us.

JOLENE
We have a plan in place. Mom is supposed to be going to an
Extendicare home in town. There's a waiting list but it looks like she'd
be in by this time next year, and I figured that was when she'd be more
. . . she'd be . . . well she'd be less . . . okay. You know, cognitively. Then
when she was off the farm, we could . . . decide what to do—if she was
too, you know, cognitively, by then, too weak to determine, you know,
what she wanted to do with the farm, then it would go to a lawyer and
there'd be . . . um . . . negotiations. Between the siblings. But Sarah
comes along—out of the blue—like literally we had no idea—and says
she'll take care of Mom. But for how long? And how, take care of her?
I mean she wasn't even part of the picture. And now she lets Mom do

whatever she wants. Go fly a kite? Sure! Paint the barn with "Robert," her dead husband? Why not? Take the truck downtown? Sure! Mom needs structure and predictability and security and Sarah isn't giving her any of that.

Pause.

SARAH
I can hear you, you know.

JOLENE
Oh for shit's sake. I don't know how this (audience) thing is supposed to work.

SARAH
I talk to them too! All the time!

JOLENE
I just didn't know you could hear me when I talked to them!

SARAH
Of course I can!

STEVEN
Can anybody—

SARAH/JOLENE
No!

STEVEN
(Whoa. Okay, then.)

KATHLEEN is there.

KATHLEEN
What are you talking about?

JOLENE
Nothing, Mom.

KATHLEEN
It's nice to see you, Jolene. And Steven.

STEVEN
Hi, Mom.

He gives her a quick hug.

JOLENE
Sorry, Mom. You were busy and we had to talk to / Sarah—

KATHLEEN turns back and sees the sandwiches.

KATHLEEN
Who made all the sandwiches?

JOLENE
You / did, Mom. You—

SARAH
Jolene did. Jolene made them.

KATHLEEN
You having a picnic?

JOLENE vaguely mumbles something under her breath.

KATHLEEN picks one up and takes a bite.

Jo, dear. You need to put something / in them.

JOLENE
I know. Yeah. Thanks, / Mom.

KATHLEEN
I mean, like, ham slices, maybe / cheese, a tomato—

JOLENE
Yeah, I know how to make a sandwich, Mom.

Pause.

KATHLEEN
Well, honey, these aren't / really sandwiches—

JOLENE
Mom. We really need to talk to Sarah about some things right now.

Pause.

KATHLEEN
Am I a thing?

JOLENE *(sighs)*.
Mom.

KATHLEEN starts to go off but turns back.

KATHLEEN
I'm kind of turning into a thing now. Aren't I?

Pause.

JOLENE
No, Mom. You're not a—

KATHLEEN
It's okay. Steven, am I a thing to you?

STEVEN

No, Mom. This isn't personal. It's business.

SARAH

How can this not be personal? This is family. If this isn't personal—

KATHLEEN

Anyone seen Tom?

No one has. They just look at her.

SARAH

No, Mom.

She stands there for a moment, uncertain. They look at her, hoping she'll leave. Lights change. Music plays as SARAH *watches her go off.*

And she strolls down the hallway like she's in a trance, puts on her coat and boots, and wanders out of the house and into the yard—like she's searching for something. And I stand and watch her through the window walking down the lane and then through the aspens and into a field. And I let her go because, through all this, she's never gotten lost. Not once.

JOLENE produces a manila envelope and drops it on the table.

What's this?

STEVEN

It's just a—

JOLENE

Document.

SARAH
What kind of document?

JOLENE
The legal kind.

SARAH
What's it for?

JOLENE
It's contesting what she said at the supper.

STEVEN
And . . . uh . . . in the will.

SARAH
On what grounds?

JOLENE
That she hasn't been in her right mind.

    Pause.

For, like, some time.

SARAH
Wow.

JOLENE
Sarah.
(slowly, with some empathy) It makes no sense that she would give the farm to you.

SARAH
Steven?

STEVEN
Honestly, Sarah? You're probably the last / person she'd—

SARAH
She drew up that will almost two years ago.

JOLENE
Yeah, around the same time she started taking dementia medication so—

SARAH
But she was fine! You said she was fine. She said she was fine.

JOLENE
Maybe she was, maybe she wasn't. I mean look at her!

SARAH
Yeah. Now. But it's all been happening so fast. It's supposed to take years! Why is it all happening so fast?

STEVEN
Sarah . . .

SARAH
She's in her right mind lots of times. Look at her a few minutes ago.

JOLENE
Asking who made sandwiches / that *she* made.

SARAH
What about / her lawyer?

JOLENE
With butter.

SARAH
Jolene, shut up. Her lawyer could—

STEVEN
Sarah . . .

SARAH
What, Steven??

STEVEN *(softly)*
She didn't have a lawyer.

    TOM *appears but he is in another scene moving planks of wood*
    around.

JOLENE
She had Tom.

    A shift. Suddenly SARAH *is with* TOM. *They are at the fort.*
    TOM *is moving planks around, hammering them in, etc., while*
    they talk.

TOM
She was in her right mind. It's even written down, the "of sound mind
and body" stuff . . .

SARAH
Yeah, but that's just you witnessing it.

TOM
Is there anything in there that suggests she wasn't?

SARAH
You mean, besides the fact that she gave everything to me?

TOM
Maybe that's the smartest thing she's ever done. Imagine if she'd given it to one of them. They'd have both lawyered up and sold the place by now.

SARAH
(Um . . .)

TOM
What.

SARAH
They're bringing lawyers.

TOM
Lawyerss?

SARAH
Well a lawyer and a real estate . . . er.

TOM
What for?

SARAH
Whaddya think? To lay out their argument and try to get me to, like— can you stop hammering and moving shit around?

TOM
I'm winterizing.

SARAH
Winterizing?

TOM
Shutting it down. Big storm comin'.

SARAH
What if they make me an offer?

TOM
An offer?

SARAH
They're going to court to contest the will. They say that Mom was suffering from dementia when she made it.

TOM
So basically they want to say that Mom would have to be crazy to leave the farm to you.

SARAH
Basically.

A pause.

Did you know?

TOM
Know what?

SARAH
That I was getting the farm.

TOM
Well I . . . I witnessed the will.

SARAH
So you knew. All this time.

TOM
I mean, it was a while ago, but yeah. Basically.

SARAH
Basically. *(thinks)* I need a lawyer.

TOM
What for?

SARAH
For tomorrow. At the house.

TOM
Tomorrow? You're not getting / a lawyer by—

SARAH
I know I'm not getting a lawyer by tomorrow!

> *Pause.*

You got any of that weed?

TOM
That might work. Get everybody around a table, with a joint, / a bong, some brownies . . .

SARAH
No, idiot. Right now. You used to keep some stashed out here.

TOM
Dude. That was a long time ago.

SARAH
You don't smoke weed anymore?

TOM
Rarely. Usually only with Mom.

> *Bit of a pause.*

SARAH
Say wha?

TOM
She says it helps her "fucked-up hip."

SARAH
(???)

TOM
That's what she calls it.

SARAH
You smoke weed with Mom.

TOM
Well, like, medicinally. And to, like, relax also.

SARAH
Have you since I've been back?

    TOM shrugs.

I can't believe it.

TOM
Okay. Don't make a big thing—

SARAH
And she swears.

TOM
When she's high? Like a fuckin' sailor.

SARAH
Wow. What else do you know?

A pause. Music starts playing quietly in the background. A wind starts.

TOM
I'll be there.

SARAH looks at him.

Tomorrow. I'll help fight your case. With you. At the kitchen table.

STEVEN is playing. The ensemble begin to create a wind—just light but growing. SARAH joins in the playing.

SARAH *(to us)*
And a wind comes up. From the southwest. Almost out of nowhere. Mom wanders the fields appearing and disappearing through trees, above a rise, behind the barn. Her coat open, talking to someone—to herself—to the wind. Negotiating, reasoning, asking.

SARAH moves off. The music continues for a bit then fades. TOM is back at the fort, holding a plank of wood, and KATHLEEN appears. TOM looks up.

TOM
Hey, Mom. You're a ways from the house.

She looks at him and smiles.

You okay? What are you doing?

KATHLEEN
Nothing.

A pleasant pause.

I thought you'd know where it is.

TOM
Where what is?

KATHLEEN
The hill.

TOM
The hill?

KATHLEEN
Uh-huh.

TOM
What you want the hill for, Mom?

KATHLEEN
I saw the fox.

TOM
The fox?

KATHLEEN
She's back.

TOM
Oh.

KATHLEEN
Do you know where it is?

TOM
What.

KATHLEEN
The hill.

TOM
I . . . I think I do.

KATHLEEN
Can you take me to it?

TOM
Uh . . . yep. Yep . . . I . . . I can. But . . . you're going to have to close your eyes while I walk you there.

KATHLEEN
Why?

TOM
It's a secret hill. How you get there is a secret.

KATHLEEN
Okay.

TOM gets up and moves toward her. The music starts up again, just dreamy, light picking from SARAH and STEVEN.

TOM
Hold on to my arm.

She does. They begin to walk—partly in place, partly in circles, taking small steps but always on the same level.

Now watch your step. 'Cause it's steep. We go around here . . . and then up over here . . . and we have to cut back here . . . and whoops, don't look down . . .

KATHLEEN
I can't. I have my eyes closed.

TOM
Right. Forgot. That's good. That's good. Keep your eyes closed.

KATHLEEN
I'm a bit scared.

TOM
It's okay. I'm right here with you.

KATHLEEN
What happens if I open my eyes?

TOM
Then you can't come to the top.

KATHLEEN
Are we almost there?

TOM
Almost. Still got your eyes closed?

KATHLEEN
Yep.

> TOM *pauses and looks at her.*

TOM
No, you don't. They're opened.

KATHLEEN *(with eyes closed)*
They are?

TOM
Sure they are. How else can you see this fantastic view?

KATHLEEN *(eyes closed)*
Yes, I see.

TOM
Now keep them open just like that.

> *A couple more steps.*

Here we are. What do you think?

> KATHLEEN *keeps her eyes shut tight. But looks around.*

KATHLEEN
It's so high.

TOM
Are you feeling the wind?

KATHLEEN
Yes.

TOM
It's beautiful up here, isn't it?

KATHLEEN
Can we go down?

TOM
Down?

KATHLEEN
On the toboggan?

TOM
Oh.

He adjusts his thinking for her.

Yep. For sure.

KATHLEEN
Okay.

TOM
Okay. Let's sit down on the toboggan. You in front, me in back.

KATHLEEN
Okay. I'm scared.

TOM
It's okay. It'll be okay. It'll be fun. You'll see. Ready?

KATHLEEN
Ready.

TOM
Here we go!

> TOM *and* KATHLEEN *go tobogganing down the hill.* TOM *moves this way and that, says, "Watch the bump," and they bump over it, tries to steer and says stuff like, "Oh, there's snow in my face," and "Woohooo." Whatever, really.*
>
> *They finish. The music ends.*
>
> *Pause.*

KATHLEEN
Again.

TOM sighs.

TOM
Means we have to walk all the way up the hill again.

KATHLEEN
Okay.

*Shift as they get up—KATHLEEN still with her eyes closed. The
ensemble start creating a storm.*

SARAH *(to us)*
I'm not sure what time the storm starts, but I wake up in the middle
of the night to shutters rattling and the house trembling and creaking.
"The wind wants you to come out and be blown forever . . . " I walk
to the window of my bedroom and look outside, and I swear I can see
Mom gardening, but when I go to check on her she's asleep.

She stands there as though looking out the window.

And find myself thinking about that fox. Where is she right now? Is
she safe? Does she have young ones? Is she real?

Another pause. She's still looking out.

The wind seems to be looking for a way in. Like it's lost and needs a
home—shelter from itself.

The sound of the storm dies away for the moment.

By morning it's a full blizzard. The first one of the winter.

*TOM is suddenly standing there wearing a suit that's old and too
small for him. He's holding a briefcase from the 1970s. Those
black and silver plastic jobs that look big enough to hold an
early VCR. He stands there looking awkward.*

TOM
Hello.

>   SARAH *just looks at him. He sees what she's looking at.*

Dad's.
From that box.
Bit small.
I don't own a suit.

SARAH
What are you doing?

TOM
What. I'm your lawyer. I told you I'd help you fight your case.

SARAH
Yeah but you're not a real lawyer.

TOM
So . . . no suit?

SARAH
You even have a briefcase.

TOM
Found it in the garage.

SARAH
What's in it?

TOM
Huh? Oh. Uh. Nothing.

SARAH
You hiding something in there?

TOM
No, like, there's literally nothing in it.

SARAH
Oh. Okay. Okay. Cool. This . . . this is gonna go great.

TOM
Hey, I've never lawyered before.

SARAH
Well we should have papers or something! Sorry. Sorry. I'm nervous.

TOM
You're nervous. I'm the one pretending to be a fake lawyer in Dad's old suit.

SARAH *(to us)*
And outside, the storm rages.

> *JOLENE and STEVEN join TOM and SARAH and they create the storm for a few seconds. STEVEN and JOLENE now join TOM and SARAH in the kitchen. The wind quiets.*

But it's coldest and quietest in the kitchen, where we wait for our lawyer guests.

> *They all stand awkwardly, saying nothing. JOLENE glances at her phone. Complete silence.*

JOLENE
What's Mom doing?

SARAH
Dancing.

JOLENE
Dancing?

SARAH
To records.

STEVEN *(half amused)*
Man, this is gonna be awkward if she comes in.

SARAH
Really? More awkward than this?

> *JOLENE doesn't reply. Perhaps she sighs. Nothing else. They stand there. JOLENE looks at her phone. Nothing. Eventually SARAH turns to the audience to say something, but JOLENE stops her.*

JOLENE
Don't you dare. If we have to sit in awkward silence then so do they. They can handle it. They've sat through the rest of it.

> *JOLENE looks at TOM.*

Nice suit.

TOM
Thanks.

JOLENE
Dad's?

TOM
Yep.

JOLENE
You her lawyer?

TOM
Yep.

JOLENE
What's in the briefcase?

TOM
Uh . . . like . . . you know . . . um . . .

STEVEN *(trying to help)*
Documents. Right, Tom?

TOM
Yeah. Documents.

> *More silence. Finally* SARAH *turns to the audience.*

SARAH
As you may have already guessed, they aren't showing up.

JOLENE
You don't know that. They could—

> *She looks at her phone.*

Shit. They've cancelled.

> SARAH *and* TOM *breathe a sigh of relief.*

Storm. Zero visibility.

> *She looks to* SARAH.

Way to go.

SARAH
What did I do? It's not my fault the storm—

JOLENE
It's all your fault. All of this.

SARAH
What?? How?

JOLENE
You think I want to have lawyers fighting it out in our family home?
And Tom as . . . as a . . .

They look at him. He adjusts his suit.

The suit doesn't even fit him, for Chrissake. You got involved and
changed everything, the plans changed, the farm changed. The town.

SARAH
We're not supposed to be fighting over the farm in the first place! Why
do we / need to have (lawyers and . . .)

JOLENE
You left the town behind. You hated this place. Dad died and you were
gone! With Chris of all people. You leave me, Tom, even Mom. You
didn't care about the farm. I was the one who stayed! Me and Tom.
We've been fine! We saw what was going to happen and we were / pre-
paring for it.

SARAH
But you don't have a life. You spend all your time trying to
handle Mom.

STEVEN
Sarah . . .

JOLENE
What are you talking about?

SARAH
You work two jobs, not including the farm! You never see your
husband . . .

STEVEN
Sarah—

JOLENE
Arrrgh. Sarah. You don't understand.

SARAH
What? What don't I understand??!

STEVEN
Just let it go.

SARAH
Let what go? What is the problem??

JOLENE
I don't—Sarah, you've been gone so long, you—I look after Mom and
the farm because—and my marriage is—we haven't slept in the same
bed for eight years. We don't even live on the same floor. Roy lives in
the basement. His recreation is playing video games with Brandon
or going to the bar. He's lost two jobs and is barely hanging onto the
one he has. And somehow Brandon blames me! *This* is what keeps me
going. I look after Mom and the farm because I don't have a life! Okay?
Shit. Okay? Sarah? This! Keeps me . . . I need this farm, okay? You
don't. You don't care and it's pissing me off that suddenly you do. And
it's yours! What the fuck? And I thought Steven was on my—I thought
he was going to help . . . make something happen but he doesn't
seem to—

Where's Steven?

STEVEN left a few lines earlier—drifted out of the room. He re-enters.

STEVEN
Mom's not in the house. She's not here.

They all look at each other.

You guys start looking for her.

He looks at the audience. Heroically.

I'll narrate.

The ensemble—except STEVEN—reassembles and begins to make storm sounds. Intermittently they call out "Mom!" and "Kathleen!" while STEVEN narrates.

TOM
Mom!

STEVEN
She isn't behind the elm that holds the tire swing that drags on the ground.

JOLENE
Mom!

STEVEN
And she isn't just over by the old farmstead house we swore was haunted.

SARAH
Mom! Kathleen?

STEVEN
And she isn't by the trees or the Quonset or along the too-far-apart aspens on the lane.

TOM/JOLENE/SARAH
Mom??!

STEVEN
And she isn't up by the fort or in the barn or the garden . . .

TOM
Mom?

STEVEN
And Tom—knowing the farm better than anyone, especially in a storm—finds Mom first.

> KATHLEEN *appears. She's in her housecoat and ranting.* TOM *sees her and keeps his distance.*

KATHLEEN
Blow! Blow, you bloody wind! Crack the house! Tear the barn away!

STEVEN
The storm feels like it's directly over the farm. Directly over Mom's field. The field that she doesn't want anything planted in. The field where she stands and screams at imaginary storms to her dead husband.

KATHLEEN
You think you've won?? You think you got me??

STEVEN
But this time the storm isn't imaginary.

TOM
Mom??

STEVEN
And there's Tom in our dad's old suit calling across time, calling through a storm to the other side—yards away that feel like years.

TOM begins to sing loudly, over the storm.

TOM
We've only just begun . . .

KATHLEEN
Blow your brains out, wind! Blow your brains out! Go on! Do your worst!

TOM's singing and KATHLEEN's shouting are uttered on top of each other at the same time. It's absurd; a strange moment of tragicomedy. TOM sings and sings.

TOM
. . . To live. White lace and promises . . .

KATHLEEN
. . . Throw everything you have! . . .

TOM
. . . A kiss for luck and we're on our way . . .

KATHLEEN
. . . I don't care anymore! I don't care! . . .

TOM
. . . Before the rising sun, we fly, so many roads to choose . . .

KATHLEEN pauses for a moment, listening.

KATHLEEN *(less convinced now)*
Blow, you crazy . . . Robert?

TOM
. . . *We'll start out walking and learn to run* . . .

KATHLEEN
Robert?

TOM
. . . *and* . . . *and when the evening comes* . . .

KATHLEEN
Robert.

> *TOM pauses. He's not sure what to say, but realizes he's wearing Robert's suit.*

TOM
Yeah. Uh . . . You okay . . . honey?

KATHLEEN
You lied to me.

TOM
I did?

KATHLEEN
Don't pretend.

TOM *(guessing)*
I did. Sorry.

KATHLEEN
It wasn't the cheating. It was the lying.

Beat.

TOM
I know.

KATHLEEN
She was a good woman. Mary-Jo was a good woman. She was hurting and alone. But she was a good woman.

TOM
I know.

KATHLEEN
She was alone 'cause of you.

TOM says nothing.

So was I.
You would have left him. Alone. Just like you did to her.

Beat.

You have to make this right.

SARAH and JOLENE are there. They stand off, listening.

I want to have another baby.

TOM
You do?

KATHLEEN
Jo and Steven are already grown up practically. And Tom's starting school. Jolene's going into grade six!

Pause.

I want to have another baby.

Beat. He looks over to SARAH, *watching from a distance.*

TOM
Okay. That's . . . that's probably a good idea.

They stand there silent in the storm a little longer.

KATHLEEN
I thought you were dead, Robert.

TOM
Me?

KATHLEEN
I thought you died.

TOM
Come on. I'd never go and do that.

KATHLEEN
I love Tom, you know.

TOM
I know.

KATHLEEN
It took me a long time. But I love Tom.

TOM
Good. That's good. I'm glad.

KATHLEEN
And I hope he finds his mom sometime.

Beat.

TOM
Me too.

KATHLEEN
I keep thinking I see her, you know?

TOM
Me too.

KATHLEEN
Maybe you can find her.

TOM
Maybe.

They both look into the sky. The wind picks up again but just briefly.

KATHLEEN
Fuckin' wind.

KATHLEEN drifts off stage. TOM watches her go. He stands there almost motionless and gradually notices the others staring at him. He and they are looking at each other . . . differently. SARAH looks to us.

SARAH
Is this what it feels like to have a long-lost brother? Was he ever lost? Somehow it feels like he's been suddenly brought to us.

JOLENE and STEVEN go to him and hug/touch him in some way.

The wind takes. It breaks. It bends. It harms and steals. But it brings too.

SARAH goes to him. They embrace. She drifts off with the others.

TOM
Long-lost brother. I am a long-lost brother.

A moment or two. A shift. Both SARAH and STEVEN have instruments they're quietly playing. SARAH and JOLENE begin to sing.

JOLENE/SARAH
Barely a breeze
I'm trembling like the trees
Made it through the spring, made it through the summer
Don't know about the fall.

It's only the air
But it's got me by the hair
And it's pushing me around, trying to take me to the ground
But I'm gonna stand tall.

SARAH
A couple of weeks later Steven flies back from Calgary with his family and invites people from the town back out for a supper. Inside this time. It's sort of to thank everybody for being there for Mom over the past months.

STEVEN
Lots of people are there. Mike shows up with his new girlfriend.

SARAH
Tom's hockey buddies show up. Jeff 1 and Gussy at least. Jeff 2 couldn't make it.

SARAH
Mom was smiling and laughing like a weight had been lifted off her in that storm.

TOM
It could also have been from the weed we smoked a little earlier.

The lights change and we turn to KATHLEEN.

STEVEN
And I catch a glimpse of Mom staring out the window, gazing at something, and then, as everyone is chatting and laughing, she calmly strolls outside and drifts away from the house.

> KATHLEEN *pauses for a moment. Perhaps she moves to another space, then calmly, deliberately raises her hands above her head and begins to fly a kite.*

JOLENE
It's Steven who first goes out and starts pretending to fly a kite beside her.

> STEVEN *goes to where* KATHLEEN *is, watches her for a second, and then starts to fly his own kite beside her.*

STEVEN
And I look to the sky and our imaginary kites and the farm and fields covered in snow and a memory strikes me. I don't know when it started but from a young age—twelve, thirteen—I realized that, when it came to the farm, Dad was more interested in Tom than me. No matter what I did, no matter how much baling, shovelling, cleaning, feeding, no matter how much interest I showed in the farm, Dad always turned to Tom. He taught him and protected him while I watched—even though I was older and stronger. And at maybe fifteen I started to pretend I didn't care about the farm. Wasn't into it. Wanted to be doing other things. Not caring—or pretending not to—is the best way to avoid hurt. So that's what I did. I mean, I guess I can forgive Dad for being an asshole to me sometimes, but Mom and Mary-Jo? That's gonna take a little more work.

SARAH
And then Tom joins in.

TOM joins. He and STEVEN frame KATHLEEN for a moment, arms raised.

And then Hans Weber.

JOLENE
And then Rick Rivera and two of his kids.

SARAH
And pretty soon everyone's outside by the barn with Kathleen flying their own imaginary kites. It's our way of saying it's okay to be in Mom's world; that hers is just as important as ours—just . . . different.

They're standing near each other flying kites. Except JOLENE.

ENSEMBLE
And it's blow, wind, blow, keep on blowin'
Scatter me everywhere
Throw me to here and there
Take what I know and make it all air.

STEVEN
Even Jolene was flying a kite.

JOLENE
No I wasn't.

SARAH
Come on, Jo. Grab a kite.

STEVEN
Yeah, there's lots to go around.

JOLENE
That's okay. I'm fine.

TOM
Here. Here, Jolene. Take mine. I'll find another one. Oh look.
Here's one!

JOLENE *(to us)*
I know what this is about. This is about me stopping going around in
circles and sittin' down in the middle of the rink and just watching for
a bit. Not literally of course. That's just stupid.

> *They all look at her for a moment. She stares back. Finally she
> relents and starts, lamely, to fly an imaginary kite. They smile or
> congratulate her.*

SARAH
I never say anything at the time but at one point I look across the yard
into the lane and I swear I see the fox. Just standing there, completely
still, gazing into the yard. But the aspens are playing tricks and when I
look again it's gone.

And as my mom is staring up at her kite, the next moment she lets it
go and watches it float into the sky, and she drifts away never looking back.

> *KATHLEEN is standing down stage looking out across the audi-
> ence at something as it rises in the air. She holds the look for a
> moment and then drifts away.*

> *They start to disperse. The music fades as people wander off.
> KATHLEEN remains and flies her kite a little longer. SARAH is
> still there.*

Rain wash me away
Tired of fighting every day
I don't want to feel the pain, memories like a hurricane
And I'm drowning in it all.

JOLENE
And Roy moves out. For now. And after he does, the first thing I do is have a family dinner. No phones. No leaving early. Just us. And Roy. And awkward silences. But it's a start.

SARAH
Two days later Chris is at the doorstep. Appears out of the blue. Like I did. And I look at him and say so so stupidly, "Chris, what are you doing here?" And he says, "I'm your husband, remember?" And it's true. He is. Sometimes you forget.

TOM
And the siblings all sit around the kitchen table.

SARAH
And I sign the farm over to Tom. And Jolene. But with the condition that Tom farms it until he can't any more and Jolene does the books. And when Steven and his family come to visit they must stay here. At the house.

And finally, once a year, we sit around this kitchen table—

STEVEN
With white bread and butter sandwiches—

SARAH
And . . . talk.

ENSEMBLE
And it's blow, wind, blow, keep on blowin'
Scatter me everywhere
Throw me to here and there
Take what I know and make it all air.

> *They all just look at each other and start the wind again. Music is playing.*

SARAH
Mom never asks about the hill again and she never drifts back to the field, but she does drift further and further away from us day by day.

> *KATHLEEN appears. She looks out at something but nothing, thinking, remembering, watching. She's neither the suffering KATHLEEN nor the KATHLEEN of old. She's simply there and beautiful.*

TOM/JOLENE/STEVEN
I don't even need it
I won't even feel it
You can never see it
It's only a breeze.

> *The three siblings fade into the shadows. SARAH stands watching her mom, who is alone, centre.*

SARAH
Where do they all go? Do they become foxes, or hares, or hawks? Do they drift away with the wind? Do they become the wind? Maybe they become the wind.

KATHLEEN
The wind wants you to . . .
The wind wants you to come out and . . .

SARAH
. . . be blown forever through a world moving too fast . . .

KATHLEEN
Through and through . . .
Through and through . . .

SARAH fades into shadows. KATHLEEN *looks out into the darkness, smiling faintly as the lights fade on her.*

End of play.

Lead Sheet

Blow Wind

Eileen Laverty

Lead Sheet

I'll Follow (Sarah's Song)

Eileen Laverty/
Jesse David Brown

You seem to lis-ten like an-gels are sing-ing Se-crets whis-pered, church bells ring-ing But all I___ hear is the wind. ___ You trav-el to plac-es I don't ___ un-der-stand Search-ing through time for a safe___ place to land And I'm___ still___ here in the wind.___

Don't be a-fraid 'cause I'm al - ways be-hind you Trust in the mo - ment and know

C   Dmi   B♭maj7 C   F

68 __ love will guide you   I'll__ fol-low if you   lead__ the way.

F Dmi   B♭/D   F

73 Some-times in life we for - get___where we're go - ing   We lose our path with-out

C   Dmi   B♭/D

76 __ ev-er know-ing   We cling to each mo-ment,   we try to re-mem-ber   but

F/A   C   Dmi

79 mem-o-ries fall___ like the leaves__ in Sep-tem-ber   I'll__ fol-low if

B♭maj7   C   F

82 you   lead_____ the way.

(Instrumental)

B♭maj7   C   F   Rit. --------

85 I'll__   fol-low

Lead Sheet

Just Over There

Eileen Laverty

love was in__ the toil,__ my tears are in__ the soil___ Oh, these

roots are deep but I no long - er hide the__ pain.__ Just o-ver

there is a road___ that leads to the high - way That-'ll take

__ me far a-way,___ far a-way__ I am

stand-ing__ tall___ af - ter__ all__ that I've__ been through

__ What's left to do__ but take the road just o - ver

there.

Don't

Lead Sheet

Love So Rare

Eileen Laverty/
Jesse David Brown

Love So Rare

Take me to — the mu - sic, — let me hear the laugh - ter—

Of my love Of my love so —

(Instrumental)

— rare.

ACKNOWLEDGEMENTS

Thanks so much to Angus and Louise at Dancing Sky Theatre for their love and dedication to theatre, new plays, and the idea of building community through the sharing of stories. Thanks to Eileen Laverty for her friendship, music, voice, and love of the process. To Skye Brandon for those first conversations way back; to Kate and Bix for being . . . Kate and Bix; to Cheryl for being Cheryl and also for asking so many goddamn questions; to Lauren, Marcel, Danny, Clax, Cam, Michelle, the amazing Jensine Emeline Trondson, and Derek for really, really liking this play; to Nicole and Josie and EVERYONE at Station Arts; to Alison Jenkins for her amazing arranging, friendship, and laughter; to poet Roo Borson for her poem and support; to the Canada Council for the Arts, SK Arts, and the Saskatchewan Playwrights Centre for their support; to Xavier, Ivan, Averie, Fenster the Cat, and, of course, my beyond compare, Melanie.

Daniel Macdonald's plays for adults include *Blow Wind, A History of Breathing, Velocity, Bang, MacGregor's Hard Ice Cream and Gas,* and *Pageant.* He is also the author of numerous plays for young people, including *These Things I Know, Flock Formations, Waking, Tragedie, The Romeo Project, Radiant Boy, Blind Love,* and *HERE.* His work has been shortlisted for the Carol Bolt Award and the Saskatchewan Book Awards. He is also a two-time recipient of the City of Regina Writing Award, the Enbridge Playwrights Award, and the Saskatchewan Arts Award. He is writer-in-residence at St. Paul's Hospital with the Healing Arts. He also teaches at the University of Saskatchewan and the University of Regina and heads the New Voices playwriting circle at Gordon Tootoosis Nikaniwin Theatre. Daniel hangs out with Melanie, little Xavier, and Fenster the Cat in Saskatoon.

Originally from Belfast, Northern Ireland, Eileen Laverty's family emigrated to Canada when she was six and, while she calls herself a Prairie girl, her Irish roots run deep. Her music reflects a range of influences, from traditional Celtic to contemporary songwriters. Laverty's track record includes several songwriting accolades, and her music has been featured in film and television programs. She has released three CDs and several singles to date. Eileen is also a dedicated teacher and coach, and a lifelong fan of the Beautiful Game—still playing when her schedule permits. She loves the outdoors and many of her songs were composed in and around the northern forests and rivers of Saskatchewan. She lives in Saskatoon with her husband, Greg Hargarten.